Confessions of a Suburban Stripper

Nicole Hellyer

CREDITS

Publisher- Corona Books
Editor-in-Chief-Jody Babydol Gibson
Front Cover Design- Jody Babydol Gibson
Photo- Author's own
Back Cover & Interior Design- Archer Ellison
Photo- Author's own

www.coronabooksandmusic.com

ISBN 13: 978-0-9792202-8-9
ISBN 10: 0-9792202-8-9

Thank you!

The following people deserve a special thanks because they have touched my life in one inspirational way or another....

First, Michael, my support, my rock; you are the only one who manages to keep me grounded. To my wonderful children: Mommy is so sorry she spent all of that time on the computer. Thank you for understanding.

To my best friends: Gina, Leslie, Ginny and Michele...you guys have always supported my decisions, and I love you for that.

A very special thanks to my FANTASTIC publisher Corona Books. Jody Babydol Gibson, Diedre Sherman, Jan and the rest of the staff YOU ROCK!

Table of Contents

Introduction

I was sitting at the bar with my girlfriends having a few drinks when one asked

"Did you want to be a stripper?"

"Actually, I wanted to be a ballerina. My dancing just ended up being pure, erotic, entertainment! I answered. We all laughed.

"No I didn't mean it like that; you just have some really good stories. You should write a book."

Who would want to hear my stories? I thought to myself. Then it dawned on me; maybe people could learn from what I have been through and perhaps my previous experiences could really help someone. I had suffered years of abuse at the hands of my inebriated father, with a passive helpless mother who was too afraid to say anything. So, I sat down with a notebook and started to write. I admit, it was much harder then I had thought. Reading over my notes made me realize that I am stronger then I give myself credit for; I no longer wear my heart on my sleeve. I am more suspicious of people and their intentions. I finally understand why you hold your friends close and your enemies closer. I have become successful even when the odds were against me.

Do I really want to put myself out there for all to see? I feel naked, defenseless with my life exposed on the pages. This book is not meant to hurt anyone or open old wounds. It is a story...after all everyone has a story. Maybe some will understand that I never meant to hurt them.

I want relief from my closet of secrets and liberation from my past. Writing "Confessions of a Suburban Stripper" was like a weight being lifted from my shoulders. I am comfortable in my own skin and want people to know that no matter what, we are able to make changes in our lives. Believe in yourself, you have so much potential, you deserve better.

So, to all of my readers, here is my story..

Chapter One
Meeting Amanda

It was September 1980. I was a tiny, five year old girl with green eyes and blonde hair. It was my first day of school. My mom picked out a white shirt, green skirt and a patterned bow to hold my ponytail and packed my lunch as I grabbed my Miss Piggy schoolbag. She walked me down the street to that big red brick building I had passed so many times before. The line to enter school started to move. Mother kissed me goodbye and off I went.

I spent the day finger painting and playing in the school yard. Mom wasn't outside at dismissal. I could not wait to see her and tell her all about my day. I came in the door and began to ramble on, noticing both my parents preoccupied in conversation. My father shouted at me to "Shut up!" He told me he didn't care about my day. I ignored him and continued to pull on my mother's pant leg. The next thing I knew I was on the floor. I had a sharp pain on my right side and felt like I couldn't breathe. My father had hit me with his crutch so hard that it sent me flying across the room. Mother scooped me up and took me into the kitchen. She gave me a glass of milk and a few cookies.

"You are okay, right baby? Daddy didn't mean to hit you. He just gets so angry sometimes" she said as she wiped the tears from my eyes.

Four years went by before I was witness to my father's rage again. My mother began the night shift when I was nine years old. I didn't see her much anymore. She was asleep when I left for school and gone by the time I came home. I had little league after school in the spring. The softball fields were just down the street from my house. I would walk to the game by myself and come home when the game was over. I don't think either one of my parents ever came to see me play. Occasionally, I would stop for a five cent piece of grape Bazooka Joe gum. It was my favorite treat. One night I heard my father screaming for me.

"Amanda, get your ass home right now!"

I left the game and ran home thinking something was wrong. Entering through the front door having to duck from a flying shoe I heard my father yelling:

"Where the hell have you been? Your game was over an hour ago!"

"No it wasn't," I replied.

That was probably the stupidest thing I have ever said. My father came at me and started to beat me with a shoe. He hit me in the face and in the back of my head. When he finally stopped hitting me, my nose was bleeding and my glasses were broken. I was sent to my room. Mom came in to check on me when she had finished work and picked up my broken eyeglasses on the nightstand. Then, she turned on the bedroom light and saw the dried blood on my face. She pulled me out of bed, took me into the bathroom and washed my face with a warm washcloth. The tears were streaming down her cheeks.

"Anthony, what the hell did you do to her? Did you hit her Anthony? Did you? You bastard!"

I had never heard that tone of my mom's voice before. Closing my bedroom door I covered my ears. The fight seemed like it lasted forever. I started coming home from school to babysitters after that incident. In the evening my sitter would drop me off at the local bar where I would find my father. Dinner was either pretzels or nachos. The bartender use to put the key in the Pac Man game so I could play as long as I wanted. I think she felt bad for me.

"Hey little girl, what's your name?"

"Amanda" I answered proudly.

"What a pretty name; my name is Jackie. Where is your momma?"

"She works at night."

Jackie shook her head and began wiping down the counter.

"Well if you need anything, you be sure to come ask for me," Jackie the bartender offered. I nodded my head and smiled.

My father would have parties at the house and lock me outside. I think that he only let me in because his friends reminded him I was out there. One night I came in and found an acquaintance of my father's rummaging through my mother's jewelry box. I waited up for her that night and called for her when she came home. I told her what I had seen and she went ballistic. She began screaming at my father.

"What the hell is going on when I am not here, Anthony? Are you having people over? People who are looking through my things? Why can't you just sell your weed from the corner like everyone else?"

Apparently, she knew nothing about us practically living at the bar or the many parties father had been hosting while she was at work. Father started working the night shift after that fight.

When I was fourteen the tables had turned; it did not take long for the kids in my neighborhood to figure out I was home alone after school. My house again became party central but this time I was the host. Every Wednesday night I had people over. Nadia brought her friend Angie with her one night. Angie and I were not close friends.

"Did you get into a fight?" Angie asked me.

"What do you mean?"

"You have a black eye" as she pointed out to everyone my bruised face.

"I guess you could say that if getting beat by your dad counts" I snipped back at her.

Everyone got quiet. There was this guy Brian from the neighborhood who was sitting on my couch.

"Your dad hits you?" he asked.

"Yes."

I was so embarrassed. The last thing I needed was to be made fun of.

"That's really not cool" Brian said to my surprise."Hey Joe, the next time her knucklehead dad comes home we are taking a baseball bat to his knees."

I didn't want any trouble and quickly changed the subject. I glared at Angie for what she had done. Brian came up to me when I was sitting alone in the corner and said,

"If you ever need to talk please call me."

Brian and I ended up becoming good friends. One Sunday, I took him to meet my grandmother. That meant a lot because my grandmother and I were very close. My grandmother would cook a five course meal when I would come over. Brian thought it would be good to talk to Grandmother about the way dad treated me. It didn't work out the way I had hoped. Grandmother said her father was the same way. She told Brian and me stories of how she would sneak out the window and down the fire escape of the house she grew up in on Saint Vincent's street. She would go to the neighborhood block parties. One night she climbed back through her bedroom window only to find her father sitting in a chair with a belt. Her sister had told on her because she wouldn't bring her along to the party. I don't think she really knew how bad things were with my dad. I didn't try to make her understand. Brian and I laughed at her stories. Grandmother loved the company. I was her connection to the outside world as she was in the early stages of Alzheimer's disease. Brian offered to take her out with us but, I was afraid. She would get so confused sometimes and I didn't want anything to happen to her.

I cheered for football and basketball in junior high school. Brian met me at every game. He was such a goofball! The way he would sit on the bleachers behind the cheerleaders and call my name. After the game he would drive me home. Brian told me everything would be fine, life would get better. He use to sing to me and try to make me laugh.

"Hold on little girl, Show me what he's done to you. Stand up little girl, a broken heart can't be that bad. When it's through, it's through. Fate will twist the both of you. So come on baby, come on over. Let me be the one to show you. I'm the one who wants to be with you. Deep inside I hope you feel it to. I waited on a line of greens and blues, just to be the next to be with you".

The seclusion started to get worse. My father switched shifts so he would be home by 8pm. As long as my grades stayed up the abuse stayed to a minimum. That was at least until I started to get phone calls. The first time my father answered the phone and it was for me he freaked. He ripped the phone out of the wall and began to beat me with it. He told me I had no right to give out *his* phone number. From then on I would cringe every time the phone rang. My friends were good about only calling at certain times but, they were human and sometimes would forget. Dad got this brilliant idea to send me to an all girl catholic school. He figured that was a guarantee that I would have no social life at all. I cried to my mom and told her I didn't want to switch schools. Mom told me change would be good for me; Boy was she wrong.

Freshman year sucked. I made some friends, but no one trust worthy. I struggled in my classes. Catholic school was different then public school the girls were very cliquey and they use to taunt each other. Talk about mean girls. There were dances every Friday night at the all boys' catholic school nearby. It was a big social event.

After weeks of begging, mom finally gave in and let me go to a dance. Two of my faithful neighborhood friends came along with me. We walked in and checked the place out. The gym was dark and packed. My girlfriend, Gianna, pulled on my sleeve and pointed Brian out to me. He was in the corner kissing some girl I had never met before! I cried my eyes out. I don't know why, we were just friends, or so I thought. Brian saw me and came over. I wanted to vomit my stomach was churning so badly.

"Hey girlie, what are you doing here?" Brian asked.

"My mom dropped me off."

"Megan, meet Amanda; Amanda meet Megan" Brian said with a giggle.

"Hey, how are you?" I said politely to Megan wanting to claw her eyes out.

"I'm good. I guess if you are friends with Brian then we'll be hanging out?" Megan answered.

I just smiled and headed for the door. I spent the rest of the night outside and never went to a Friday night dance again. I was so sad that weekend just bumming around the house. My friends called but I didn't feel much like talking. Nadia, her mother and her brother came to pick me up from school on Monday. Nadia's mom, Pam, knew about the lousy relationship I have with my parents. She tried to talk to me about it, but it was awkward.

"I have a surprise for you guys" Pam was smiling.

"What's up mom?" asked Nadia.

"Girls, freshen up your makeup, we're going for a ride!"

Nadia and I dug through our bags and pulled all of our makeup out. We put each piece on the backseat of the station wagon. There's nothing like a best friend. Nadia's brother, Rob began to tease us.

"Put a sock in it Rob, because you are going with them" Pam said.

"What? Come on mom!"

Pam turned up the radio and began to sing. She was so goofy.

"Where are we going mom, really?" asked Nadia.

"You will see soon enough."

I noticed we were getting onto Interstate 95, heading south into the city.

"So, how do I look, Nad?"

"You look beautiful my darling Amanda."

We giggled and sang for the rest of the trip. Finally, we entered a parking lot in the city.

"Okay guys, I felt bad because Friday night didn't go so well. I want to make it up to you; so, you guys are going to be on Dance Party USA!! !!" Pam screamed.

OMG! She walked us into the building where the show was being taped. The line to get in was long, but we had tickets! Nadia's brother smiled at a girl in line and they started chatting. We were hoping he met someone because then he would leave us alone. He came over and introduced her as Kelly Ripa. She was cute with blonde curly hair and big dimples. Rob said she was a regular on the show. I didn't watch it that much to be honest with you. I overheard Kelly telling Rob she was from New Jersey. He was acting so cool. Kelly was talking to Rob about a recent audition she had for All My Children. I couldn't help but to interrupt.

"That is my favorite soap opera! Good luck to you" I offered.

Kelly smiled. The line was starting to move. I had never been on a television set before. There were cameras everywhere. The lights were white and hot. It was so exciting. The music started and people didn't waste any time hitting the floor. I hoped it would never end. Nadia was laughing. I felt lucky to have such a good friend. The staff organized a lip sync contest. Kelly, the girl Rob made friends with in line, was a finalist. She was singing to Mind Over Matter and did pretty well. Rob was impressed. The hour and a half we spent there flew by. My cheeks were sore from smiling. I couldn't wait to see the show on TV. Nadia's mom was waiting in the parking lot. We ran out and gave her a group hug and a big kiss. She deserved it.

It wasn't long after that when I started sneaking out my bedroom window to meet up with my friends. We would play cards, smoke weed and drink beer. It was the only time I ever felt like I could relax. I would watch other girls get trashed and head into the woods with one of the neighborhood guys. Like everyone didn't know what was happening. Brian showed up one night I was out and had the nerve to hit on me!

"Hey, can we talk for a minute?"

"About what?" I asked him.

"Listen Mand, I know you feel what I do. I miss you."

"Knock it off Brian! I am not falling for it this time and I'm not going there with you. Not now, not ever."

I said goodbye to my friends and headed home. When I walked

into homeroom the next day everyone got quiet and when I sat down they all began whispering. Lisa, who sat in front of me, said to Michele, who sits next to her

"I can't believe she did that to Breanna. What a loser, no wonder she has no friends."

I wasn't exactly sure what they were talking about but I knew it involved me. Finally, my friend Leslie came up to me and asked

"What happened with you and Brian last night?"

"Nothing, why" I answered.

Well, apparently Breanna had a crush on Brian and had been trying to date him for some time. Last night, someone who was out with us must have reported back to Breanna that I was talking to him. Whatever, I so did not have time for this petty bullshit and felt tortured until graduation because of that crap. Brian and Breanna were off and on. I no longer spoke to him. He did call every once in a while and stop by my house but that was as far as it got. I stopped hanging out with girls from school and stuck to my neighborhood friends. It was safer that way. Everyone knew me as the girl with the coke head dad. I would just sit in the circle waiting for my chance at the bong. Life sucked. Boys wanted to get in your pants, girls couldn't wait to stab you in the back. They were missing the big picture. The fact is we are all in this together.

I tried so hard to see the good in life. Sometimes it just wasn't there.

I had three close friends through all of this: Jen, Gianna, and Nadia. They knew me better than anyone else. They knew it was rare to see me out. They knew what the occasional black eye and busted lip were from. We were each other's saviors. Jen had a baby boy senior year; her boyfriend ditched her when she was three months pregnant. Gianna's dad died junior year; he was drunk and smashed into a telephone pole while driving. Nadia was raised by a single mom, who was never home. We all tried to be positive. We told each other that we were going to make it out of here and things were going to be alright. We had big plans.

Graduation day was finally here! I couldn't wait to get the hell out of high school. All of the unexplained bruises I had and the spontaneous crying. I think my teachers all knew about my shitty home life. They just couldn't wait until I wasn't their problem anymore. While my friends headed down the shore, I hit the books and enrolled in a summer course at the local community college. I paid for it out of my summer job savings, wanting to get ahead of the game. The fact that I was going to college made my dad go nuts. He was up my ass like you wouldn't believe and doing everything in his power to make me give up. One Monday, I came home from class and my father was having lunch in the kitchen. I went and got a folding tray table and sat in the living room to start my homework.

"You need to get your shit out of here. I am making lunch in the kitchen then I am coming out here to watch TV" he said.

I picked up all of my things and set my homework up in the kitchen. My father came into the kitchen and said:

"Will you just get out of my way?"

"Where the hell would you like me to go?" I screamed back.

He knocked all of my books to the floor. I bent down to pick my books up and my father kicked me in the face. I fell to the ground and he began to kick me in my stomach. My mother came down the stairs screaming.

"Anthony, what the hell are you doing? Stop it, stop it right now!"

But he didn't stop. In fact he began to kick me harder. I had my car keys in my hand, flipped my mace open and started to spray him in the face. I had enough. I swear, if there had been a gun in my hand I would have shot him without any thought. I realized then that I had snapped.

Needing to get out of there, I got in my car and drove off. Returning a few hours later to find all of my things were thrown across the lawn. My mother came out the front door crying.

"I love you, you know that right? You have to believe me. I love you but you have to leave."

My father came to the front door screaming,

"It's either her or me."

I will give you one guess who she picked, and it wasn't me. I saw smoke coming from the back yard and went to check it out. It was a bonfire of all my childhood memories; photos, stuffed animals, trophies, academic awards all up in smoke. Dropping to my knees I gathered up what I could. Mother pushed me back to my car. She kept saying she was sorry, I know she couldn't help how she was. Mother was a text book co-dependant. She couldn't function without my father.

"Mom, I know you love me and I understand."

I shut my trunk. The problem was I had no money and no where to go. Distraught, I went to Nadia's house where I spent the night. I woke up and went to school the next day.

"What's wrong Amanda? You look so sad" asked Lindsey, a girl I had become close to at school.

"Where do I begin?"

"It can't be that bad."

"Well, I grew up in an abusive house where my dad beat the crap out of me on a regular basis. My mom was never around much and when she was, had to tend to my drug addicted father. Yesterday my dad hit me for the last time."

"Did you kill him?" asked Lindsey.

"You would think I did after everything he has put me through, but I left voluntarily. I honestly have no idea what I am going to do now. I can't live out of my car."

"Why don't you come home with me after class? I have an extra room. Maybe I can help you out. Don't worry, it will be Okay" Lindsey smiled and wiped a tear from my cheek.

I went to Lindsey's after school. The townhouse was beautiful. I loved it. The house felt so comfortable. When you walked up the stairs into the living room there was a fireplace in the corner. The sun was strong coming through the big window in the kitchen and there were sliding glass doors that led to a balcony. From the balcony you could see the common grounds. There was a jogging path that led through the park and to the playground. I was so excited. Lindsey took me to the room that would be mine. It smelled a little stale as she was using the room for storage but it was a good size and had a bathroom attached. The bathroom had a Jacuzzi tub. I had never seen one up close before. The house was in a nice neighborhood, a beautiful park setting. Nothing like I was use to but everything I wanted it to be. Lindsey and I sat and had a glass of wine. We discussed the living situation and my money problems.

"Listen, I don't want you to worry about money right now. We will work something out" said Lindsey.

"Do you know anyone who is hiring? I can pretty much do anything: cook, clean, wait tables, whatever."

"Let me talk to my boss and I will let you know."

This was great! My life is turning around. I went up to my room and started to unpack. That night was the most restful sleep I had in years. No yelling, no hitting. I could take my time and do things at my own pace. The next morning was beautiful. I came out of my bedroom and Lindsey had a place set at the table for me.

"Good morning Sunshine. I toasted you a bagel. There is orange juice and cream cheese in the fridge. We have time. Remember, we are only ten minutes from school. So, do you want to come to work with me after class? No pressure, just come and check it out."

"I don't see why not."I answered.

It was so nice to sit down and take my time. I didn't have to worry about someone yelling because I was in their chair. Or that I ate their food. Lindsey and I packed up our things and went to class. I seemed to breeze through my class work that day. Lindsey was trying to copy. Slacker! Class ended and we walked to our cars.

"So do you still want to follow me to work?" Lindsey asked.

"I guess I'll check it out."

It didn't dawn on me until I pulled up that Delilah's Den was a Gentlemen's Club. When we walked through the doors the first thing I noticed was the "gift shop". The gift shop contained things like lingerie, liquid latex, stiletto heels, pasties etc. The place was exactly what you see on TV: the runway, the huge mirrors and neon lights. I sat down at a table in the corner and started to play with the menu. I nervously scanned the room. My stomach started to hurt.

Lindsey came over with her boss, Mike. Before he shook my hand he flashed a snap shot of me.

"Don't get upset, I take pictures off all my girls for the private party portfolio. Hi, I'm Mike, the manager of Delilah's. Lindsey told me about your situation. You are cute! I don't see why you couldn't dance. It wouldn't hurt for you to lose about ten pounds."

My mouth must have dropped; this from the man with the Dunlap over his belt.

"Pay him no mind, Amanda. He just likes to hear himself talk, right Mike?" fired Lindsey.

I thought that he was a little strange.

"You don't have to dance if you don't want to. There are other things you can do here but you will make more money if you dance" she confirmed.

I couldn't believe it. It was 1pm and the place was jamming, men were drooling all over their lunch. I guess in my mind strippers only came out at night.

"So, what do you want for lunch? It's on the house" Lindsey asked.

"Are you going to eat with me? Or just leave me here in the corner?"

"We'll eat together, but if you want something I have to go get it, silly."

I guess I just didn't want to be left alone. We had lunch and Lindsey took me to meet some of the other girls. I was shocked when I walked into the dressing room. There was a mirror on the makeup table with lines of cocaine cut. I tried not to stare. I couldn't believe how young some of these girls were. A few glanced over and said "Hi". There was an older red head sitting at a makeup mirror putting mascara on. She glared at me and rolled her eyes. Lindsey said not to worry about it. Some of the older girls get upset when new girls come in. They think they are going to lose customers.

"Hey, I scheduled you for the virgin dance class tomorrow." Lindsey said.

"What the hell is a virgin dance class?" I asked.

"It is a class where they teach how to strip, you big dork!"

Driving home that afternoon I wondered what to do and had to admit I felt a lot more comfortable than I thought I would at the club. Do I go back? Will people think less of me if they find out what I am doing? The girls there did not look trashy like I thought they would have been. TV can be so stereotypical. I popped open a container of Ben and Jerry's and turned on MTV. Lindsey came home a few hours later.

"So, what did you think?" she said sitting down next to me.

"I don't know; I'm a little nervous about the whole thing. What do you think? Do you think I will be any good? And what about the weight comment Mike made? Do you really think I'm fat?" I asked.

"Don't listen to Mike, Amanda, he doesn't know what he's talking about. You're funny and cute. The guys will love you. And you'll make big money cha-ching!" Lindsey giggled.

"Okay, I'll go to the class tomorrow. If I don't like it I'll look for something else."I decided.

"That sounds fair." Lindsey answered.

I went to my bedroom and got ready for bed catching a glimpse of myself as I passed by the mirror in the bathroom. Maybe Mike was right, maybe I was fat. I suddenly felt nauseous. I turned on the bathroom water so Lindsey wouldn't hear me and began to vomit. When I was through I cleaned up and brushed my teeth. I lied in bed thinking what if I go through with this and begin to hate myself? I will be the only one to blame.

Chapter Two

First Time

I went to the club as scheduled the next morning.

"Oh my God, is that you Amanda?" someone said from behind me. I was shocked when I saw Christy. Christy and I went to grade school together.

"Christy, I can't believe it! How are you? How is your mom? I never thought I would see anyone here that I knew."

"Well, here I am. If it makes you feel any better, you're the first person in two years that I have seen here that I know. My mom and dad got divorced. Dad moved to Texas with my brother. Mom does okay, but she couldn't afford to put me through college so, I teach girls to strip for extra cash."

It was funny seeing Christy here because she was kind of a tomboy in school. She played the drums in band class and was the only girl on the football team. I think she was as shocked to see me as I was to see her.

"I've been dancing since senior year. My mom and I moved to

New Jersey. I'm only right across the bridge from here. I figured no one would ever find out. I met a great guy. He works in construction. We have an apartment in Cherry Hill. I just bought a new car."

"What does your boyfriend think about your dancing?" I asked.

"He doesn't say much. As long as no one touches me he's cool with it. Besides, I'm making more money than he is."

Four other girls entered the room. They were all cute and young. We went around the room and introduced ourselves.

"Hi, I'm Lori. I'm from Mt Laurel, New Jersey. I have a daughter named Ava. I am going to school to be a radiology technician and decided to dance because the money is good and the hours are flexible."

"Hi, my name is Sue. I honestly think it is curiosity that brought me here. I grew up around here and noticed this place is always packed. I figured I would find out what the big deal is about stripping."

"My name is Jamie. I have two boys and recently got divorced. I use to be a stay at home mom but now cannot afford to do that anymore. I need a flexible schedule to work around my kids."

"I'm Sheryl. I am here because I need the money. I lost my job bartending and this is the first place that called me back."

Christy started by showing us one of her routines. She was good and could actually get her nipple into her mouth. I was impressed. Unfortunately my own doesn't reach. I wondered if you could write breast implants off on your taxes if you need them for your job. Then,

Christy showed us moves on the big brass pole. I was intimidated. She was swinging and hanging upside down. We all started to laugh and cheered each other on as each of us tried it out. It was fun! Every girl had a different style. You could pretend to be anyone you wanted.

"So Amanda; You seem to be the cheerleader type. What are you doing here?" Lori asked.

"Well, if you really need to know, I had a crappy childhood and my mom picked my dad over me. Now I'm on my own and I have no money. Otherwise, trust me, I wouldn't be here."

Christy let us play on the pole and walk on the stage and catwalk to get comfortable. She put on some tunes and did some cool moves to Whip It and Brick House. She had to end class in an hour to open the club for lunch. Christy and Mike invited all of us to go eat and watch some of the other girl's routines as class ended. I stayed, I wanted to wait for Lindsey anyway.

We left the club and met up with some friends at a local bar. I loved drinking and dancing. It was such a release. I didn't have a boyfriend at that time, and didn't want one. Lindsey was funny; she kept trying to hook me up with all of these people. Tonight was no exception.

"Amanda, this is Trevor."

I was going to kill her.

"Hello," I answered.

"Do you want to dance?" asked Trevor.

"Sure."

Trevor was cute. And to my surprise he could dance.

"I haven't seen you before. Are you new around here?"

"Pretty much; I'm really just starting to get out more."

I looked up and my heart sunk. Across the room was a face I knew from years ago. I had a horrible flashback: It was a fall afternoon. I was at Nadia's house. Her brother was having friends over for a football party. Pat was one of those friends. Pat came up behind me in the kitchen and pulled me into a bedroom. He pushed me down on the bed and put his hand over my mouth. The tears streamed down my face but that didn't stop him. He unzipped his pants and pulled down mine. He pressed his chest to mine. When he was done he got up and walked away. I ran out of the house. I couldn't get home quick enough. I sat in the shower and could have cared less if the water burned my skin off. I never told anyone. I hadn't seen Pat again until today. I heard he went to juvenile hall for raping another girl younger than me later that same year. I was 15 at that time. I excused myself from Trevor and made my way toward the bathroom to throw up. I gained my composure, put some cool water on my face, stepped out of the bathroom and rounded the corner when Pat grabbed my arm.

"Hey you, long time no see."

"Not long enough. Do you think I don't remember what you did to me?" I pushed Pat into the wall.

"Wait a minute. We were kids, besides I had the biggest crush on you."

"And that makes it okay? I haven't been the same since."

Just then Lindsey approached.

"Hi, I'm Lindsey, I don't think we met?"

I pulled Lindsey with me as I walked away.

"What is wrong with you?" Lindsey asked.

"Just stay away from him. He's bad news!"

"Okay, Mand, I trust you, chill out." Lindsey replied. We went back to our friends and played a game of pool.

The next day Lindsey was helping me come up with routines for work. You should see some of the things she had in her bag. Besides the stiletto heels, she had this cute bow tie with a matching G-string and a plaid mini skirt with a white button down oxford.

"Guys love that school girl routine" Lindsey said. She wore a pink sequin braw underneath the white oxford that tied in the front. That was really cute, especially with ponytails and a lollipop.

"You'll be fine, don't be so nervous."

Lindsey gave me some tips like: putting blush on the inside of my boobs to make them look bigger (I was only a B cup). She told me guys think it's hot when you put liquid latex on your nipples for a wet look, and I thought it was only used to apply pasties!"There is no wonder why it's a best seller in the gift shop". Lindsey said.

"Once you get your own customers you should try to get them to book private parties. You make bonus money that way. Or if you get your customers to buy a bottle of Dom Perignon, that is extra cash too.

The key is once you get the party started you get the guys credit card and you start running a tab. You have to keep him ordering."

Everyone met back up at Delilah's the following night for an amateur dancer show. A few of the girls from the virgin class were there. We hung out and chatted. I didn't get up on stage that night. I wasn't ready yet. Everyone else was good. I needed to practice the pole. Lindsey took me into one of the private party rooms where there was a lone pole. She told me to have at it and take all the time I needed. I found the switch that turned on the purple lights. My friend Kevin poked his head in the door. He came in, unbuttoned his shirt and tried to swing on the pole. That didn't go so well. He could always make me laugh. We went out for drinks after the show.

"Hey, you guys need to use the buddy system; they found a girl dead on Maple Beach. She was only 24 years old. She was shot in the back of the head" Kevin said.

"Do they know what happened or who did it?" I asked quickly scanning the room.

The perpetrator could be anyone in here. How scary is that? It made me wonder if dancing was a smart thing to do. I was munching on wings when one of the guys we were with wanted to go check out the murder scene.

"You're crazy!"

"Come on, the crime scene tape should be down. Let's go check it out."

The girl murdered was named Dana Bernstein. I didn't know her, but a few of my friends did. Dana used to hang out at the local bars and strip clubs. Rumor had it that she was an escort, if you know what I mean. The cops think one of her "Johns" killed her. We walked through the woods until we hit the river. It was a cool summer night. The stars lit up the sky. My friends were running around acting stupid, trying to scare each other. I sat down on the beach and just watched the waves come in. This place seemed so peaceful. You would never think that this was the last place someone was alive. I wonder if she had any idea what was about to happen to her.

"Hey, I heard she was a hooker," Bob said.

"Even if she was Bob, that doesn't give anyone the right to murder her!" I snapped.

I walked along the water. There were still tiny pieces of yellow tape blowing around. Bob thought he was funny running up behind me, chasing me all the way to my car. That was enough! I got the chills. The yellow police tape was a reminder that you are never safe. I vowed never to let my friends go any place alone again. I tossed and turned most of the night; that place creeped me out. I woke up the next morning to Lindsey running her hands through my hair.

"Hey there; you must have slept well. You were snoring."

"Honestly, I felt like I was having an anxiety attack." I answered.

"You should have woken me up; you know I have a pill for that."

"I did it to myself; after you left last night a few of us went to check out Maple Beach where that girl was murdered."

"Well then, I don't feel bad for you. I can't believe you would go there. You do know they haven't caught whoever shot her yet? You deserve to get the shit scared out of you. Anyway, do you want to go shopping with me today?"

"Sure, I could definitely benefit from a new comforter."

I loved to shop, I just couldn't afford it. My room was taupe with white trim and white window dressings. Lindsey and I went to the mall. I found a really cute burgundy and gold comforter set. Until I turned it over and saw the $425 price tag. Yikes! Who can afford to pay that? We checked out a few stores before I found a light blue and white comforter set. It was cute and in my price range. Clearance for $99, you can't beat that. I was so excited.

After our shopping, Lindsey and I went over to TGI Fridays across from the mall. Lindsey's fiancé was coming home from a NASCAR race. He was going to meet us for dinner.

"Hey Ladies", Chuck called out as we walked into the bar area."Amanda, this is John" he said introducing us.

Chuck and Lindsey said they would be right back, they had to run out to the car. No doubt that was a set up.

"So, how do you know Chuck?" I asked.

"I know him from high school. He's a good guy. You go to school with Lindsey?"

"Yes. She also just helped me get a job at Delilah's."

"Have you danced before?" John asked.

"No, and I am so nervous" I answered.

"Don't be. You're hotter than a lot of the girls down there."

"You go to Delilah's?" I asked.

"I have been there before with Chuck to pick up Lindsey. So, do you want to get together sometime?"

"Sure, I'm living with Chuck and Lindsey now so call me there."

Chuck and Lindsey returned to the table. We ate a great dinner and then went home. My stomach was churning thinking about work the next day. It seemed that vomiting was the only thing making me feel better. I felt guilty but it wasn't like I couldn't stop doing it if I wanted to.

I was so nervous, leaving for work around 1pm the next afternoon. I needed to throw up at every traffic light. Lindsey went along to cheer me on. When we got to Delilah's it was pretty crowded. I made my way into the dressing room, found an empty locker, and slowly got ready. Maybe time would stop. I couldn't get over all of the drug use in the locker room. Guess you can't blame the girls if it's what they need to do to get them through their routines. Lindsey came in behind me and asked

"What's your name?"

"Are you freaking kidding me? I thought to myself.

"Seriously; what is your stage name?"

I never thought of one. HMMM! I had an idea. My favorite character from TV was Amanda Woodward, you know Heather Locklear on Melrose Place. She was such a bitch, but she could hold her own. I yelled

"Heather."

"Okay, Heather, five minutes and you're on!"

I threw up in the trash can. Some of the girls started to laugh. I heard another say "Amateur". Lindsey told them to shut up as she helped fix my makeup. I wouldn't have been able to hold it together if it wasn't for her. I heard my music start and I went out. Bon Jovi's song "Runaway" was what I opened with. I thought it was fitting; wearing a black mini dress with thigh high boots and a platinum wig, once on stage it wasn't so bad. I got lost in the music. There was something fun about being sexy, flirtatious. My hands were sweaty as I grabbed the pole. I swung around and turned upside down and occasionally made eye contact with some of the people in the audience. That was the longest three minutes of my life. After finishing the set I made rounds on the floor. Some of the men were gross with missing teeth and long nose hair. Others were surprisingly clean cut, business type. The guys would make their little comments as they put cash in my G string. At that point, I realized I was going to have to develop a strong self esteem to make it in this world. I can do this. I already had a deep seeded hate for men, thanks to my no good father. What the hell, I don't have a problem taking their money. A guy tugged on my G string and I turned around.

"Hey, I would like to pay for a lap dance for my friend here, it is his birthday and he's a virgin."

The guy handed me a $100 and winked. I took his friend by the hand and entered the back room. I sat him down on a bench, handcuffed his hands behind him and turned on the radio, straddling him until his face turned red. I rubbed up against him and let my hair fall all over him. I turned around and shook my ass in his face, then flipped over and touched myself. Suddenly I felt wet on my side. I looked at my customer and he had a strange look on his face. Oh no, his dick made its way out of his pants and he sprayed come all over my side.

"I'm so sorry, you just excited me, and I couldn't control myself."

"It's fine really" I said removing his handcuffs.

He was so embarrassed, he ran out of the room. I got some towels and cleaned up. My first night wasn't so bad. I walked out with $400 cash after tipping the DJ, house and bouncers. I didn't know one had to do that. Thank God Lindsey told me while packing up to leave. You have to tip the DJ otherwise he won't play the music you want; you have to tip the house because they let you work there and you have to tip the bouncers because they look out for you. Lindsey told me I could tip the house mom too if I wanted a good schedule, he-he.

Off from work the next day I slept in and it was nice. I didn't get to do that with my parents. I decided to just hang out at the house and began going through my stuff. I wasn't exactly sure what I had in the way of belongings. Living out of trash bags was not the way to go. I also had to go get some cool costumes for my other routines. The phone rang and it was John, the guy I met last weekend. We made plans to go out that night. I was so excited I called Lindsey. John was so cute. He wanted me to pick him up at his house for a trip to Atlantic City.

I got to John's house and he was sitting on the porch waiting for me. He walked over to my car with his shirt unbuttoned. I wasn't sure what to think of that. He came over to the driver's side door.

"Hey girl" John said, "Do me a favor and move over."

I was a little put off because I normally don't let people drive my car. He must have figured out I was annoyed because he quickly apologized and said

"I think girls should be chauffeured. I promise to be careful."

I took a deep breath and moved over. We headed to Atlantic City, NJ. I had never been there before. It was so cool; all of the lights, the people, the cha-ching from the machines. It was overwhelming. John handed me a twenty dollar bill and told me to go have fun. He was going to play at the black jack table. I ventured around the casino. I found a dollar slot machine I liked and put in the whole twenty, hit for eighty and lost it all. That was fast. I need to learn that you should quit while you're ahead. I wandered back and found John. He looked up and smiled. I stood behind him and watched him play. I don't know how to play black jack. I was not exactly sure what was happening. Lights started flashing and sirens were sounding. John turned around and kissed me. Security came and whisked us away. He had hit for thirty thousand dollars. Wow! Security took us to a back room. John had a million papers he needed to sign. I couldn't believe they take taxes out right away. The government doesn't miss a thing. John was so excited. He cashed out and wanted to get something to eat.

"So, what is your favorite food?"

"I love Italian, but it's your night. I'll eat where ever you want."

"Italian is good. There is an Italian eatery inside the Showboat."

We got there and they seated us immediately. The place was really nice with a cozy table in the corner. There were white candles, white linen table cloths, it was a beautiful ambiance. I opened the menu and almost died. The cheapest dinner was $25 and that was for pasta and broccoli.

"So, do you have any plans for your new found wealth?" I asked.

"Well, I'm probably going to put a down payment on a house. I also wouldn't mind a new ride," John answered.

"That's great! I wish I were that lucky," I said.

"It really isn't that much after taxes," John countered.

"Anyway you look at it, it is way more then I have now."I answered.

We had an incredible dinner. The food was the best I had ever eaten. I felt like a princess, at least until the bill came. John had the audacity to ask me to split the bill with him. He just hit for a mint of cash. We used my car and my gas to come down here and stingy bastard won't even foot an eighty dollar dinner bill.

"I can't believe you John!"

"You know what? You're just like the rest. You're nothing but a whore!" John exclaimed. I stormed out of the restaurant. I started to cry, got my car from the parking garage and went home without John. When I got back to the townhouse Lindsey, Chuck, and a girl named Summer, from work were there. They could tell I was upset. I told them what had happened. Lindsey said

"Don't worry, Honey, you can do so much better."

"He is an ass for acting like that" Summer said.

I knew they were just trying to make me feel better but I went into my bathroom to vomit. I had to sit for a while after becoming lightheaded and dizzy. My stomach hurt. I had laxative pills in my medicine cabinet and took a few of them before returning back out into the living room. Summer said,

"I will make you feel better. Let me tell you the story about my ex, Carlos. I met him out at a bar. He was so nice. He was a real gentleman.

He would open doors for me and pull my chair out at the table. He would buy me nice things. Then I found out I was pregnant. You would have thought the sky was falling. Carlos said the baby wasn't his and we went our separate ways. I started dancing after my son was born. I had to pay the bills and keep food on the table. Now Carlos is constantly complaining about child support saying it is too much."

Carlos was a nurse in the military. He could afford to support his son. He just didn't want to.

"Do you believe that when we went to court for support he wanted everything accounted for? He even had the nerve to bring a list of ghetto daycare centers because they were cheaper then where my son already went!"

Summer said I reminded her of herself. She used to wear her heart on her sleeve.

"People are out for themselves. No one really cares about you. You cannot be naïve of people's intentions. You will learn and, you will become stronger or you will fail."

She was a little rough but she was right. The phone rang and Chuck answered it. It was John.

"How dare that little tramp leave me in A. C. ! I had to have my brother come down and get me."

"Yo, John, first of all you need to apologize. Amanda told me what you said to her."

"Chuck, you are kidding right? Whose side are you on?"

"Look, she's a nice girl and you were way out of line."

Summer took the phone from Chuck and told John to go fuck himself. It was nice having someone else stick up for me. Lindsey, Summer, & I broke open a bottle of wine and sat in front of the fireplace until late.

Summer and I worked the same shift the next day. The club was crowded. After my set, Summer introduced me to a group of regulars sitting in a corner booth. Men bond over the strangest things, football, food and strippers. Who would have guessed? Craig was one of the guys who stood out. He was dressed in a nice suit, smiling and waving to everyone as he walked by. Summer said he was a latex salesman with a lot of cash. He was a great tipper if you paid special attention to him. There was another guy at the table named Eric.

"Hey Summer, are you still doing private parties?" Eric asked.

"Not usually; why?"

"We are having a bachelor party for one of the guys at the firehouse and we would love to have you as our star attraction."

"I guess I could for you. But you need to pay me in advance. That is why I don't do private parties anymore. It was a pain in the ass trying to collect from drunken men" Summer said.

The party was scheduled for Saturday night. I went along to make sure everything was Kosher. I didn't get a warm and fuzzy feeling from

Eric so I asked one of my friend's, a cop named Kevin, if he would join the festivities. Kevin was cute. He was 6'2", 210lbs. I loved a broad shouldered man in uniform. He had a shaved head that felt good to rub. He was a lot of fun, and never tried to pressure me for any more than being "just friends". Kevin picked me up and we headed to the firehouse in New Jersey where the bachelor party was being held.

"So, how did I get the honor of escorting you this weekend?" Kevin asked.

"Oh, I don't know. Maybe I just thought you were a good guy" I teased.

"Okay, you got me there. I was just really surprised to hear from you."

Kevin and I had a few drinks and danced. Around 9pm Summer showed up and started her set. I went over to the make shift bar they had at the firehouse.

"Hey, what's a girl got to do to get a drink around here?" I said to the guy behind the counter.

"Oh my God, heaven is missing an angel."

"Is that the best you can do?"

"Well, why don't you give me a chance so you can find out?" So, what can I get for you?" he asked.

"I'll have a cosmopolitan, please."

"How about trying this out? I am going to put a new twist on an old favorite?" The bartender said while he was mixing behind the counter.

Just as he handed me my drink Kevin came up and put his arm around me. The bartender practically dove across the counter trying to get my drink back. I thought that was strange.

"Hey, I gave you the wrong drink!" the bartender yelled.

"This one is fine."

The guests were getting a little rough with Summer. I saw a few guys pull her from the table she was dancing on. Kevin headed over to calm things down. I started to feel strange. The room started to spin. I was so dizzy. The bartender came out from behind the bar and put me over his shoulder. I tried to call for Kevin but nothing came out of my mouth. The bartender carried me downstairs and put me on a couch. He started kissing me; I couldn't keep my head up. I started to cry, but he wouldn't stop. He began to push my skirt up. Just then, Kevin came flying down the stairs. He punched the jerk in the face and knocked him to the ground, picked me up, and carried me out to the car.

"Summer, let's go!" Kevin called out.

My head hurt so badly. Everything was fuzzy.

"What the hell happened in there?" Summer asked.

"That dickhead behind the bar put something in Amanda's drink!" yelled Kevin.

"Oh my God, honey, are you alright? Wait until I get my hands on

Eric. I will find out who that kid was"

Summer said as she pulled me up against her in the back seat.

"I promise I will get you through this. You'll stay with me tonight"
she promised.

"No she won't, answered Kevin, She needs to go to the hospital."

"I'm not going to the hospital, Kevin; I'll be fine please I just want
to go home before I puke!"

Kevin was worried about me. I hadn't seen that side of him before.
I just thank God Kev got to me in time. We dropped Summer off at her
apartment.

"Kev, you will take care of her right?" she asked.

"You know I will" Kevin answered.

He carried me into the house, helped me get changed and brought
some ice water to the bedside table. He held my hair as I prayed to the
porcelain God. Kevin tucked me in and lied down on the floor next to
the bed. He slept there all night. It has been a long time since someone
genuinely cared about me.

I had to work that next afternoon but felt like I was suffering from
a bad hangover. I saw Eric at the bar, the regular who asked Summer to
do that private party. I grabbed him by the ear and yelled

"What was the name of the kid behind the bar?"

"Get off of me you crazy bitch!" Eric said as he elbowed me in the
chest.

"He drugged me you asshole."

"You're crazy; you don't know what you are talking about, screamed Eric, Who's going to believe a whore anyway?"

The club owner heard the way Eric was talking to me.

"Hey, you don't talk to any of my girls like that, the owner said, bouncers, escort our friend here outside and take his gold card away."

It's about time someone stuck up for us. The rest of the night went okay. I dressed up like Pocahontas and danced to Jungle Love. I finally mastered the pole that, at one time, had intimidated me. I had my favorite bouncer tie a sling swing atop of the stage so I could swing from it. They are hard to use but they look SO cool. The customers went nuts. I collected some great tips. My boss even came up to me and told me he was impressed at how much I had improved. When I came home from work I couldn't sleep. So, I put on a kickboxing tape and went to work. Maybe my boss liked me more because I was losing weight? Besides that I need to be stronger to protect myself from jerks like Eric. It became very apparent that I had to look out for myself.

Summer came over the next afternoon. She brought her son over to meet me. They brought water ice and soft pretzels.

"I feel so bad about what happened the other night" Summer said.

"Please, I am over it. It wasn't your fault. You didn't try to hurt me. Just promise, no more private parties."

"Hey, I am going to take a ride to the beach. Do you want to come? We need to get a way" Summer smiled.

"That sounds good."

With all of my life drama I hadn't had much time to relax.

Chapter Three
Let's Hear It for the Boys

I could not wait to escape. All of the things I had been dealing with went running through my head. But you know what? I survived, yes, I am a survivor. All of the heartache and all of the hurt just proved to me that people are not always what they seem. Now was my chance for a new start and I was going to take it. After loading my bag in Summer's new SUV I asked her

"So how can you afford such a nice ride?"

"Let's just say my tips have been really good lately."

"You mean Craig's tips have been really good lately?" I responded.

"Whatever" she said as she hopped into the driver's seat.

"Seriously, what is going on with you two? I'm getting the feeling that he is not just a customer."

"Really, he *is* just a first-class customer."

"If you say so, just be careful with the clientele" I warned.

"Now look who's giving who advice" Summer laughed.

It was a beautiful day at the beach with a warm breeze blowing across the water. We found a spot right in front of the lifeguards. Anthony was so cute. Summer pulled him along in a wagon that contained all of his sand toys. After we lathered him up with SPF 70, I helped him dig a huge hole and fill it with water. It had been so long since I played with a child. He was very happy. I sat down and flipped through my magazine. I love the beach. Kids were playing football in the sand. Summer pulled Anthony along on his boogey board. Anthony said he was hungry so we packed up and headed to the boardwalk. I was glad it wasn't crowded. We took Anthony on rides and had some pizza. He fell asleep in his stroller on the way back to the hotel. Summer tucked her son in and gave him a good night kiss. Anthony was such a good boy. I missed out on that mother-child bond when I was little. Summer's own mom met us at the shore and agreed to watch Anthony while we hit the bar. There was a cool place right on the beach. It didn't take long before two guys came over and bought us drinks.

"Hey Ladies, are you here with anyone?"

"We just came to play darts" I answered.

We tried to ditch them but, they followed us like puppies. I had just started throwing my hand when in walked Craig and his friend.

"Did you invite them? ' I asked Summer.

"No, but I did tell him where I was going this weekend."

The two guys hitting on us must have gotten pissed off because when I came back from the bathroom they were gone along with my purse. God Damn It! I ran out into the parking lot and they were leaving in their white Neon.

"Don't worry, I have money" Craig offered.

"That wasn't the point; it's that all my stuff is in there. My license, credit cards, cash and keys are gone."

Craig's friend Chris tried to make me feel better.

"Hey, I saw your act at the club the other night and thought I was great."

"Are you kidding me? I just got ripped off and that is all you can say!"

I split from Craig and Summer, finished up my dart game, and was ready to go back to the room.

"Can I at least walk you home?" Chris asked.

"I guess." I answered.

As we turned the corner there was that white Neon. I ran up to the side of the car and my purse was sitting on the floor of the backseat. I tried the door but it was locked. Chris said,

"Do you really want your purse?"

"Of course I do!"

Chris kicked the window in and pulled my purse out. The car alarm was whaling and we ran. What a rush! We jumped off the boardwalk and down into the sand. It wasn't long before we heard the police sirens. We were laughing so hard I started to cry. That adrenaline rush made me so horny. I climbed on top of Chris. We started to kiss. It was so intense. I took off his shirt then he took off mine and started to suck on my nipples. I pulled out his dick and started rubbing it up and down. I could hear Lindsey say

"Just think of it as an ice cream cone." I giggled and started to ride him. He held my boobs as they bounced up and down. I leaned into him and he grabbed onto my ass and squeezed my cheeks. He pushed me off and came all over himself. We cleaned up as best as we could and walked the beach until the sun came up. Chris took me back to the house and asked for my number. I gave it to him.

"Can we meet for dinner tomorrow night?" he asked.

"I guess I owe you one for getting my purse back." I practically skipped to the room and then slept for a few hours before we went back to the beach. Summer was sitting at the breakfast bar when I came out.

"So, what happened with you and Craig last night?" I asked.

"I went with Craig to help him find a hotel room. And we ended up having a fight. Do you believe he said I was getting a belly? He said I needed to work out more."

"He must have brass balls! Has he checked himself out in the mirror lately?"

My cell rang, it was Chris. He wanted to meet at the Italian restaurant on the boardwalk at 5pm. I was so nervous and really liked him. I relaxed on the beach for a few hours. Then strolled the boardwalk, trying to find something to wear and I found a cute baby doll dress at a boardwalk store. It was light blue with scalloped edges. I started to feel nauseous walking back to the room. It was probably my nerves. I turned the water on in the bathroom and forced myself to be sick. It is the only thing that helped.

"You look hot! Are you excited?" said Summer.

"Oh my God, you don't even know."

"You guys had sex, didn't you?"

I smiled as I grabbed my purse and went out the door. Summer came out to the balcony and yelled,

"I want to hear all about it when you get back!"

I got to the restaurant and Chris was already seated. He looked so proper in khaki shorts and a yellow polo shirt. Dinner was great, and we loved being able to watch the waves come in while we sat. We didn't run out of things to talk about either which was a positive. Chris began to question me about Delilah's; that made me feel uncomfortable.

"Dancing is just a stepping stone for me. I have goals, I want to finish school."

Chris kept on pressing and wanted to know if I got turned on while I was dancing. He asked if I had ever slept with a customer. Then he had the nerve to ask me if I would have sex with him and his girlfriend. His girlfriend!

"Didn't we just have sex last night?"

"Well, she wanted me to have sex with you first and see if I liked it. She wants to come up tonight and join us for a threesome."

My heart sunk. I got up and walked out. Chris followed me saying he was just trying to be funny but I found nothing funny about it.

"Slut!" he shouted.

I just kept on walking. I was so tired of having my feelings hurt. Summer was on the deck drinking wine when I got back.

"How did it go?"

"Horrible, he was so nasty when I didn't feed into the game he was playing. He wanted me to have sex with him and his girlfriend. When I said no, he called me a slut!"

"What a creep!"

"It is my own fault. I shouldn't have gotten my hopes up."

"Don't talk like that. You'll find someone who appreciates you for who you are" Summer said comforting me.

The next morning we packed up to go home. School was starting soon and there were still some things I needed to buy. The ride home was quiet. My mind started to wander. I still wasn't sure if I made good choices this far. Maybe I shouldn't be dancing. I felt so alone sometimes, even when there was someone sitting right next to me. Summer dropped me off at the house. Lindsey and Chuck weren't home. There was a note on the fridge door that said, 'Went to California to get married! Wish us luck! 'Are you kidding me?

What is the matter with these people? I made myself something to eat.

After I cleaned up I went to the community college to get a booklist.

I wandered around campus like a little kid. It was a nice day. There is

an art museum on campus so I went and checked it out. There were so

many beautiful pieces. One day I will have my own art collection. It

may not be all original work, but it will be a collection all my own.

I got in the car and called Christy to see if there were any open

shifts at work. My books were going to cost me more than I had

planned. Christy said 5p-9p tonight was open. I told her that I would

be in. That is the one thing that is nice about dancing; you just pick up

extra shifts when you are running low on cash. I bought a cute flowing

white piece with matching fish net thigh highs and had a Tori Amos

gig put together. No sooner had I walked in the club doors when they

were calling me to the stage. I liked the pole, rather than working the

floor. On the pole you didn't have to make much eye contact and get

slobbered on and molested like working the floor. Some of the regular

biker guys were in tonight. They were good guys; I just wouldn't mess

with them. My new routine was a hit. Tori Amos knew what she was

talking about: 'Why do we crucify ourselves, everyday?' those words

of hers echoed in my mind. I heard some jerk in the audience tell a

new girl that her ass was too big to be dancing. She ran into the locker

room. Before I could open my mouth to say anything one of the biker guys told jerky boy that if he insulted another woman they would be pulling a broken bottle out of his neck. Needless to say, that gentleman left the building in a hurry. I went to check on the new girl. Her name was Roxanne, she was sweet with rich dark hair, and blue eyes. I told her she needed to get tough. Not every guy is going to be nice. If they know you are weak they will pick on you. You have to be stronger and smarter than the customers. After calming Roxanne down I packed my things and went on my way. I was so tired. I went home and camped out on the couch. Let's see what movies are on. After flipping channels I found something to watch and started to feel anxious. I made it into the bathroom just in time, falling asleep on the bathroom floor.

In the morning I counted my tips and put the money in an envelope, got a shower, and had some breakfast, before heading back to campus to buy my books. The line for books was around the building. I needed to go shopping for new clothes; maybe to the mall if I ever make it through this line. I heard my name being called. It was Colleen, a girl from high school. She was pregnant, very pregnant. Oh God, don't let her see me. I really don't feel like seeing anyone right now but too late, here she comes.

"Hello stranger! How have you been? Have you seen anyone from school?"

"I'm alright. I've seen some people from school in passing but no one that you used to know."

"I was pregnant at graduation but I didn't tell anyone because I was embarrassed. No one liked my boyfriend and now I understand why. He's gone and I had to move back in with my mom."

"I am so sorry, Colleen. Guys are jerks! I hope everything works out for you."

She gave me her number and told me to call so we could get together. I wouldn't bet on it. Colleen was friends with that girl, Breanna; the one that tortured me over Brian. I don't see a new best friend in Colleen's future.

As luck would have it, they were letting more people into the bookstore. I couldn't wait to get away from Colleen. Don't get me wrong; I'm not usually a bitch. She just couldn't give two shits about me in high school. So now I am suppose to care?

Anyway, how cool is this? Some of the books I needed were available as used. They looked like they were in good condition too. I ended up saving fifty bucks. SWEET! I could go to Macy's and hit the clearance racks.

When I got back to my car there was a flyer on it. The flyer said MTV's show Singled Out was coming to a club in northeast Philly. That sounded like fun. I called a few friends and went to the mall to buy something to wear. Macy's and Express had some really cute things on sale. I found a quiet corner seat at the food court in the mall and had enough money left for a slice of pizza and a soda. Across from me was a girl about my age having lunch with her mom. Envious, I ease dropped on their conversation. They were so cute; mom was asking her daughter what she needed to get ready for college, then told her what she *should* have. They were going to look at space savers, clothes and microwaves. My mom couldn't function well enough mentally or physically to take me shopping. We really didn't spend anytime outside of the house together, never went on family vacations or to an amusement park. She never giggled with me over a boy that I liked. It hurt so much inside. Like a void in me that I don't think will ever be filled.

I went home and got ready to go out excited about tonight! I had never seen a live TV show before. I went to pick up my girlfriend, Gianna; we hadn't gone out in a while. It was like home at her house. Her mom, Sue, would critique our outfits.

"Are you guys seriously going out dressed like that? What are you thinking? Why don't you rent a few movies and hang out? You will get into less trouble that way."

"No, way! Why don't you come with us?"

"You are so funny, you know I am too old for that stuff" Sue answered.

Nadia came over and it was like a reunion of sorts. The more the merrier. The line to get into the Ninety Fourth Aero Squadron was long. This cute guy came up to me and handed me a ticket and said he wanted me to be on the show! Are you freaking kidding me? They were calling for everyone with a pink ticket to go to the front of the line. I kissed my friends good bye and went to check out the deal. The announcer told us we were all picked to be in a pool of women for the bachelor to pick from. There was a woman running around with a makeup brush powdering people's noses. The adrenaline rush was wild. I started jumping up and down. It was nice to see Gianna and Nadia in the front row. They were cheering for me! On Singled Out, the hostess who is usually Jenny McCarthy, asks the group of contestants a list of questions. Based on the bachelor or bachelorette's answers is how you move up in the game. If your answer is different from what the bachelor/bachelorette would have chosen you are eliminated. Of course, Ms McCarthy wasn't available this evening and there was a stand in. She was cute with short, platinum blonde hair. She had a tiny frame, very similar to Jenny. Here is a selection of questions that were asked of me on the show:

SINGLED OUT QUESTION AND ANSWERS

1. Cheerleader or chess club?

Cheerleader! I took a step up! Wa Who!

2. College or high school?

College, I took another step forward!

3. Lake or ocean?

Ocean, this is way too easy.

4. Vanilla or chocolate?

Chocolate, (like I had to think about that.)

5. Truth or dare?

Dare, Oh my goodness, there is only like ten of us left.

6. Early riser or night owl?

Night Owl, if I wasn't I wouldn't be here.

7. Italian or Mexican?

Italian, it is part of my heritage.

Blonde or brunette?

Blonde, I moved up! Oh my God, there is only two of us left.

Light rain or thunderstorm?

Thunderstorm, we need a tie breaker!

MTV Plugged or unplugged?

Unplugged, I lost. Sorry, I can just get more into unplugged tunes.

Well, I got a tee shirt for my trouble. It was fun. The bachelor wasn't that hot anyway. Someone said they recognized him as a local construction worker. No big loss. I found my way back to my friends. The club was so packed we had to get as many drinks as we could when we made it to the bar. I got so toasted I passed out across a table. One of the bouncers noticed me there and dragged me outside. Bastard left me on a bench. I tried to wobble to my car. Unfortunately a local law enforcement official had different plans. He told me if I tried to put the key into the ignition I was going to jail. I decided to sleep it off in the backseat of my car. I don't know where the hell my friends were. I figured they would come back to the car when they were ready to go. I woke up at 4am alone and cold. There was no one around and the parking lot was empty. I was still drunk , opened the driver's side door of my car, and vomited. I took a chance and drove home. I was so nervous. I felt like I couldn't focus on the road. I made it home and crawled into bed.

A few hours later I woke up to Summer banging on my front door. I let her in and went back into my bed.

"What the hell happened to you?" she asked.

"Why, what do you mean?" I answered.

"Your car door is open and there is vomit down the driver side door. Then there is a trail of more vomit leading to the house."

NICE, my neighbors must be so pleased. I looked around and there were clothes starting at the front door leading all of the way to my bedroom. I guess I stripped on the way in; force of habit (he-he). Summer lectured me about driving drunk. I know I shouldn't have but all I wanted to do was go home. I got lucky this time. I'll never take a chance like that again. Summer wanted me to hurry up and shower. We were going furniture shopping for her apartment. I got dressed and we went out.

"Where do you want to go?" I asked.

"Let's just check out the places around here."

"I'm hungry, can we just eat first?"

We stopped at IHOP and then went to a furniture store nearby. Summer found everything she wanted there. We have way different tastes. She is more contemporary, I am more casual. The saleswoman came back with a total of like seven grand! Holy smokes, I couldn't afford that. Then I heard Summer ask the saleswoman if she got a discount for paying cash.

"Girl, where is all of this cash coming from?"

"Come on, I've been saving for a while."

My ass, I'm sure Craig was behind this purchase as well. The money we made wasn't that good. Summer set up delivery for her furniture. We both had to go to work that evening so we just went in together from there.

Work was crowded so, I walked straight to the back and chatted it up with a few of the girls before heading onto the floor. There was a guy at the bar that caught my attention. It was a guy I knew from high school. This was awkward. What do I do? I hadn't danced in front of people I knew yet. Maybe he won't see me. I kept walking until there was a tap on my shoulder.

"Hey girl, what are you doing here?"

Oh my God!

"Hi, Bob, how have you been?"

"Are you working here?" he asked.

"I am" I answered.

I had 30 minutes before I had to go on stage. Wonder if I can get him out of here before then.

"So, Bob, what are you doing here?"

"My brother is getting married. We're having a party for him in one of the back rooms. A girl named Roxanne is our dancer."

"I know Roxanne. You will like her she is really sweet."

"That's good. I'm still going to keep an eye out for you."

"Great, but you have to keep your hooting to a minimum."

He laughed and headed to the back room. I went back into the locker room to get ready. The girls were passing around some weed. Boy, I needed that tonight! My set started with Janet Jackson's song Nasty. Bob saw me and sat stage side. He was cheering like a nut. Who does that? I use to have a crush on Bob. I just never told him. When I made my rounds on the floor Bob approached me to do a body shot. We really were not supposed to have mouth to anything contact on customers but there were no bouncers around. Bob put sugar on my shoulder, sucked on the lemon, took his shot and sucked on my shoulder. I returned the favor, it was kind of hot. Bob stuck his number in my G string. I knew I wouldn't call but he was fun to play with. I did really well on tips that night and met Summer outside. She was next to her car talking to Craig. I asked Summer if she thought he was for real with all of his money and his big plans. I can't believe he isn't already married.

"Actually, he is married but, he's going through a divorce. He has an infant daughter as well, that's why he's going through the process slowly."

"Is Craig getting divorced because of you?"

"No; not at all!"

"And you believe that?" I asked.

Summer just smiled. I knew Craig wasn't her type. He just spent a lot of cash so he could be around her. We put our things in the truck and drove home. Summer's son was with a sitter that night so she dropped me off at home and left. That was good because I had to get my shit together for school. After all, I couldn't dance forever, right? I bought new laxatives to help me lose weight. They were not supposed to upset your stomach. I will give them a try.

Just as I was hitting the sheets someone came in my front door. It was Lindsey. She was divorcing Chuck.

"But, you just got married!"

"Yeah, but I caught him in our hotel room with some whore."

Uh oh, this wasn't good.

"What can I do to help?" I asked trying to make her feel better.

I thought she would tell me it was okay. Instead, Lindsey wanted me to help her gather all of Chuck's things and put them in the

fireplace. I got it all: pictures, CD's, DVD's clothes. What didn't
fit in the fireplace I was to put out front by the curb. Lindsey went
outside and poured bleach all over everything that was left. It gets
even better. Chuck owned a towing company. Lindsey and I drove
over to the company and moved the three tow trucks he had to a
remote storage facility. I was laughing so hard my stomach hurt. Then
I thought about everything we did. Chuck is a big dude and he is
going to be pissed. Lindsey and I went home. I locked my bedroom
door and went right to bed.

The next morning there was pounding at the door. Chuck wasn't
in Cali anymore. I got up and started getting ready for school. I
heard Chuck yelling and apparently so did the neighbors. I peeked
out my bedroom window and there were two cop cars. Lindsey and
Chuck were now fighting on the front lawn. I went out to try to calm
Lindsey down. Chuck started freaking out about his trucks. The cops
said Lindsey had to take him there. Otherwise, they were going to
arrest her for grand larceny. I told Lindsey just go with the cop and
give him all of the keys. The second cop escorted Chuck in the house
while he gathered what was left of his things. Chuck said he deserved
what she did to his stuff and wasn't going to press charges. The cop
said that was a good idea. He told Chuck to just go and cut his losses.
Lindsey was crying when she came home. I felt bad for her. All she
ever wanted was to be happy. I sat in bed with her and rubbed her

head until she fell asleep.

I had to get to school. The parking lot was already full when I got there. I hated being late. That meant I had to park all the way out by the baseball fields. I made it to my composition class in time. There were still seats left. I didn't recognize anyone in class. That was good, all fresh faces. No one needed to know I wasn't always from Yardley. A cute guy sat down next to me. He was a small guy, maybe 5'6", blonde hair, blue eyes and he smelled fresh. I don't think I heard one word my professor said. I was busy staring. After class my new friend introduced himself as "Mike". We walked out together. I played it cool. We chatted for a few minutes but I had to get to my next class. I told him I would see him next class and started to walk. I looked back and smiled and he was still watching me walk away. YES! I think I skipped all the way to microbiology. There was no one hot in that class. I heard every word that professor said.

I had homework the first day. That was a bunch of crap. I didn't have to work that night and I think Lindsey needed moral support anyway. When I got home she was still in bed. The curtains were drawn not letting a speck of light in. I called Summer to come over and help cheer Lindsey up. We ordered pizza and I made popcorn. Lindsey just sat on the couch wrapped in her comforter. Her eyes were real puffy. I don't think I ever saw her look that sad. Poltergeist was on, I loved that movie. I know I am a big dork. At least the movie changed the mood in the house. We hung out and talked all night. I think it made Lindsey

feel a little better.

Chapter Four
Home For The Holidays

Thanksgiving was coming up fast. It was a big, fat reminder of how alone I was and missed my grandmother. She was at her best this time of the year while baking cookies for two months straight, along with hand pressed and stuffed homemade pasta. It was when I was with her that I felt comfortable and at peace.

"Hey you, are you daydreaming again?" Lindsey asked.

"No, what's up?"

"Do you have any plans for Thanksgiving?"

"No, I have no plans to do anything."

"So, how about we cook here? ' she questioned.

"Really?" as she chewed on a carrot. We could invite a few girls over from work that don't have plans. No one should be alone over the holiday."

"That sounds like fun. Let's go shopping after we put together a menu."

"Menu? It's thanksgiving! Where did you grow up? Thanksgiving is turkey, corn, mashed sweet potatoes, cranberry sauce and pumpkin pie. Let me just see how many people want to join us before we buy food."

Lindsey had six definitely yes's for our Thanksgiving feast. We went food shopping and ran into a guy she knew who wanted to make plans for tonight. It was the Wednesday before Thanksgiving, the biggest party night of the year. We took our groceries home and got ready to go out but I was still feeling a little bummed. In the back of my mind I knew I was never anyone's priority. That hurt. Honestly, it made me want to drink. There were knots in my stomach and I felt like I was going to puke since it always felt better after that. We pulled up out front of the bar and there was a long line to get in. Lindsey and I mingled and made our way to the front. The bar was hopping. I found a seat at the bar and started to drink. There was a guy sitting next to me I knew from the club and as we chatted it up he bought me a few drinks. I was starting to feel better. Lindsey came over and took me by the hand and led me to the dance floor. Spinning around and singing I noticed Lindsey getting a little fresh with a big, bald headed guy. Of course she was nice enough to send his friend my way. He was cute, in a baby face sort of way.

"Hi, my name is Mickey" he said with a smile.

"Like the mouse?" I answered.

"You are a funny little girl."

We danced and drank until early in the morning. Lindsey and I walked out to the car and my new friend Mickey came up from behind me and took my keys. He put me in the passenger seat. Lindsey and the guy she was hooking up with got in the back. Mickey was driving like a nut. I held onto my seat. He was doing 90 mph down an "S" curved bend! I couldn't get out of the car quick enough. Thank God we weren't that far from the house.

Lindsey and her new man were making out all over the furniture. I headed right for my bedroom. Unfortunately, so did Mickey.

"Hey, so what is up with you?" he asked.

"Nothing really, it looks like you are stuck with me" I said pouncing onto my bed.

"I wouldn't call it stuck. But I do hear you club girls are dangerous."

Oh no, I knew he would go in for the kiss. What the hell, like I have something better to do. Surprisingly enough we were on the same page when it came to sex. There wasn't going to be any. Just when I thought it couldn't get any worse Mickey started to tell me his life story. I just wanted to go to sleep.

"You see, I dated this girl for two years and she broke up with me last month."

"Do you want a drink?" I interrupted.

"Yes, that would be great. You are a pretty cool chic. I can't believe you 're alright with this."

I walked out into the living room to be greeted by a great white ass and some moaning.

"Come on Lindsey! I yelled. "You couldn't even make it to the bedroom?"

I stopped for a second. His wagging balls were huge!! The boy was hung like a horse as he caught me looking and smiled. He didn't miss a beat during their doggy style.

"I can fuck you too if Mickey isn't doing the job, he said."

"I'm okay, thanks."

I took two beers out of the fridge in the kitchen and made my way back into my bedroom. When I got there Mickey was asleep. God Bless America. UGH… the bastard is lying on my favorite comforter! I tried to get it out from under him but he was snoring. Damn it! I'll have to get another blanket out of the closet. Finally, I can get some sleep.

When I woke in the morning the guys were gone. Lindsey was as chipper as ever. She was basting the turkey in the kitchen.

"Somebody got some." I chanted.

"Didn't you get any?" Lindsey asked.

"No, I have class."

"Bullshit!" Lindsey responded.

"Yeah, you're right. He wouldn't give it up."

"I knew it had to be something like that."

I turned on the Thanksgiving Day parade and started slicing pepperoni.

"Hey Lindsey, Do you have stuff to play poker?"

"Yes, up in the attic there is a fold up table and chips. A poker game sounds like fun."

I brought everything down from the attic and set it up in the living room. People were starting to arrive. We had a good hour left before the turkey was done so we sat down for a quick game. I loved girl talk. Spending time together meant getting updated on everyone's life. Leslie started the conversation:

"Ok girls I have news but you're all going to think that I'm stupid if I tell you about it."

"Come on, we would never think you were stupid. Even if we did we would never tell you, so spill it."

"You know that guy Dave I was dating?" Leslie asked. "Well, I never thought anything of it when he asked if he could just call me when he wanted to get together. He said he traveled for work and was out of town a lot and called me the other night to go out. I went to pick him up at the usual house he is out front of. I must have been early because he wasn't there yet so I went up to the door and knocked. This guy came to the door and said Dave doesn't live here. In fact, Dave lives two doors down with his wife and kids!!!"

"No freaking way!" said Denise."I met him and he seemed really nice."

"Of course he seemed nice. It was because he was getting some on the side."

We all started to laugh. Ding! It sounded like the turkey was done.

We all took a seat in the dining room and held hands and bowed our heads to pray. It was so nice to have company. I really was afraid of ending up alone.

Friday was the only night I was working over the holiday weekend. The club was slow. I guess all those married men had to be home with their families. I didn't care since that just gave me time to study. Finals were next week. There was this guy named Keith who started talking to me at the bar, saying something about wanting to drown his sorrows. He wasn't a regular at the club. In fact, I had never seen him here before.

"I don't know what is the matter with me, said Keith. " I treated my girl like she was a princess and she still left me."

"Relationships are tough."

"Why are you so nice? You could be walking around making money. Instead you are standing here listening to me whine."

"Sometimes all we need is someone to listen." I replied.

Keith stuck a $50 in my G string. I smiled and went about my business. The club was still slow so I got my things together to leave and didn't bother to get a bouncer to walk me out, which was my normal routine. I had just put the key in my car door and I heard, "Hey!" I was so spooked I dropped my keys. I looked up and it was that guy Keith from earlier.

"You scared the shit out of me Keith! What the hell are you doing back here?"

"Well, I overheard the bouncers talking about how all of the girls parked back here. I didn't mean to scare you. I just wanted to see you again."

"I'm working next Tuesday and Wednesday night. You can see me then" I snapped annoyed.

"No, I want to see you outside of the club."

"I'm sorry Keith, but I don't date customers." I opened my car door and put my bag inside.

"You don't understand. I'm not like those other guys. I'm a good guy. My family has an awesome business. Just look at the hot ride I have."

"Keith, I'm sure you're a great guy. I am just not interested."

Keith came at me and grabbed me by the arm.

"You're hurting me Keith! Let me go!"

Thank God one of the bouncers came out for a smoke.

"Hey, you! Get the hell off of her!"

Jerry yelled as he ran toward us. Keith took off running. I was okay, just a little shaken up. I got into my car and dropped my keys again. I don't know how much longer I can do this.

The next two weeks were finals at school. I was so happy break time was coming. I didn't know what to do with all of the extra time. I picked up some open shifts at the club. Keith was hanging around trying to get my attention. After days of ignoring him, he finally got the hint. I told Lindsey what happened that night in the parking lot and she told me I needed to toughen up and be more aware of my surroundings. She was right; I was still a little naive. I met Lindsey for lunch after our last final.

"Congratulations, I'm so proud of you for finishing the semester. You really had a lot on your plate and you didn't give up. You go girl!" Lindsey said.

"You're embarrassing me." I whispered.

"I have a surprise for you."

"What did you do?" I asked.

"We're going to New York City for New Year's Eve!! !" Lindsey screamed.

"Do you know I have never been to New York? I have never seen a Broadway show or the Statue of Liberty."

"Well, I can help you check Times Square off of your never been seen list!"

I was so excited. When we got home I went on line to get directions and checked out photographs of the area and the hotel we were going to stay at. Lindsey and I sat by the fireplace on Christmas Eve and watched "It's a Wonderful Life". If that movie doesn't inspire you, than nothing will. I fell asleep shortly after the movie was over and awoke with a gold box in my hand. It had a red bow tied around it.

I opened it and there was a beautiful four leaf clover charm on a gold chain. My eyes started to tear.

"Now wherever you go, luck will be with you" said Lindsey from the doorway.

"I didn't know we were exchanging gifts."

"I saw it and thought of you" Lindsey responded.

"I did get you something."

"Oh my God, it is so cute!" Lindsey said as she pulled a red, green and cream throw blanket out of the silver bag. The blanket had "Friends Forever" embroidered on it.

"Now you'll have a throw blanket for all of those nights you fall asleep on the couch and I'm not here to cover you." I said.

Lindsey started to cry. I walked over and gave her a hug. Everyone needs a good friend.

It was New Year's Eve day. I was so thrilled to be going to New York. I packed a bag and got a shower. When I came out of the bathroom Lindsey was sprawled out on my bed.

"Hey, what would you think if we got a ride to New York instead of taking the train?"

"I don't care, why?" I asked.

"There is this real estate guy I know named Marty, he called today and said he booked a room right in Times Square for tonight. He said we could stay there instead because it is closer then the room I booked."

"Does he want any money? Because I know it has to be expensive."

"No, he's just a nice guy." Lindsey responded. Hum, no one is that nice. It was then that I got the feeling something was up. But what the hell, it is New Year's Eve and I am going to New York!! ! Wahoo!!!

"Amanda, Marty is here." Lindsey called to me.

I got into the back seat of Marty's Jaguar. Nice ride. He was way older but seemed very nice. Lindsey and Marty talked the whole way to New York. Truly glad otherwise I would have felt obligated to keep the conversation going. I can't stand silence. The bridge going into New York was HUGE. We had to find a place to park and certain streets were already blocked for the evening's festivities.

"I don't freaking believe it. They already blocked off the street the hotel is on." said Marty.

"It's alright, Marty. We can park and walk."

We passed parking lots that were $110 per night, $80 per night, finally Marty stopped at one that was $72 for 24 hours. We parked there. Wow, that is really expensive. There were people everywhere. It was freezing outside. Lindsey and I walked arm in arm following Marty. We passed two other girls walking arm in arm as well, they blew us kisses. I guess they think we're a couple. We laughed and finally made it to the hotel. Marty went to check in. The lobby was black marble and white chairs, very modern. We took the elevator to the fifth floor. The room wasn't far down the hall.

"So this is it", said Marty, as he opened the door.

"This is tiny" remarked Lindsey.

"Tiny? It cost me $650. This is New York City and it is New Year's Eve".

"I know, I was just saying."

"Here is a key to the room. I have to go meet someone. Get your butts to Times Square and have fun. I will see you guys later" Marty answered with an exit.

Lindsey was right. The place was really small. The bathroom was half the size of the bedroom. I opened the blinds in the window and said hello to a brick wall.

"Welcome to New York" said Lindsey.

"They don't have windows here?"

"It's a city. Some buildings only get light on one side because there are buildings on the other three sides of them. Now let's go check out Times Square!"Lindsey squealed.

I grabbed my backpack and filled it with bottled water, snacks, a scarf and my camera. It was already 10:30pm. We had to go if we wanted to be able to see anything. Lindsey and I began to run. The crowd came to a stand still about two blocks from where we were staying. You could still see the tower in Times Square; it just looked so far away. I couldn't believe the energy in the city. I felt like a million bucks! I started to jump up and down and scream. Everyone waiting around us was so friendly. The girls next to us were from Michigan, on the other side of us they were from Boston. That was so cool. There was a laser light show and a concert. We couldn't hear that well where we were. People started to scream, the countdown had begun. I got such a knot in the pit of my stomach. 10-9-8-7-6-5-4-3. . 2. . 1......

HAPPYNEWYEAR!!!!!!!!!!!!!!!!!!!!!!!!!!!!!!!!!!

There were fireworks and an explosion of ticker tape. People were hugging and kissing. Music was playing, champagne corks were popping. People were jumping from store overhangs. It was amazing. I just stood and stared. Lindsey and I walked through the crowd to get closer to the ball. It was so bright. We ducked into a pizza place that was there. We sat down and had something to eat. We also got a chance to warm up before venturing back out in the cold. When we walked outside it was like a different place. All of the people were gone. The mess was all cleaned up. It was quiet. There was suddenly a ton of taxi cabs available. We walked past people lined up waiting to get into clubs. I have to say the architecture in New York is beautiful. The buildings are like nothing I have seen before.

"Hey, Lindsey, why don't we move here?"

"Are you kidding me? You have no idea what it costs to live here, do you?"

"I am guessing that means it's expensive to live here?" I answered.

"Boy, you really did live a sheltered life."

We stopped in the bar that was at the hotel. It was so classy. No bar stools, just couches and pub tables. I felt like I didn't belong here. It was 4:30am when Marty re-appeared. I was ready for bed. Lindsey wanted to stay out with Marty. I kissed her Happy New Year and went upstairs to the room.

I woke around eleven a. m. There actually was some sun bouncing off of the brick wall view that the room had. Lindsey and Marty were nowhere to be found so I'm beginning to think that I was just brought along for the ride. That's okay. There was a free trip to New York out of it. I got dressed and went out to explore and was like a kid in a candy store. The huge store fronts, fashion, the prices...whoa...the prices. So I definitely cannot afford Barney's. My pager went off. It was a New York City exchange, it was Lindsey.

"Hey, start heading back it's time to go home."

"Alright, I'll meet you at Marty's car".

Marty and Lindsey seemed very tight during the ride home. Lindsey had her hand on his knee and she was giggling which makes me worry. She has been bouncing from guy to guy since her and Chuck broke things off. I was beat when we got home but straightened up the house and did some laundry. It is so nice to have a "do nothing" day.

Chapter Five

Murder On The Main Line

The next morning, I made French toast, like my Grandmother taught me. Lindsey and I ate breakfast together. We even drank orange juice from wine glasses. It felt rich. I was in a great mood, cleaned up breakfast and sat down in front of the TV. The soap opera "All My Children" was on. Holy Crap! It's that chick Kelly, from Dance Party USA. I don't believe it. I guess she did make it to TV after all. Good for her! Summer came over unannounced. She wanted to team up with Lindsey for some retail therapy. I would have loved to join them but I was running low on cash. They were not gone long when the phone rang. It was Summer; she was crying so hard I couldn't understand what she was saying. Lindsey got on the phone and told me to put on the news. They will be back at the house in a few minutes. There was an interruption in the regular broadcast for a breaking news report. Murder on the Main Line was plastered across the bottom of the screen.

"A woman in her lower Merion township home had been murdered by an intruder. She was found drowned in her bathtub. Her baby girl was in her crib down the hall" said the reporter.

How horrible was that! I thought to myself. The woman was an attorney of some sort. I assumed that this person was a relative of Summer's the way she was carrying on.

Summer and Lindsey came in the front door silent. Summer sat down on the couch.

"What is going on?" I asked.

"The woman who was killed is Craig's wife" Summer said.

I never knew Craig's last name or I may have figured that out on my own. The reporter did say she lived with her husband. I thought Summer said before that they were divorcing. I guess he still lived there? Summer's cell rang. It was Craig, he wanted to meet. Summer told him to come to our townhouse. It didn't take long for Craig to show up. He looked like hell.

"What happened?" I asked.

"I don't know. I came home and found her in the tub."

"I thought you said you were not together?" I asked.

"We were trying to work things out for our daughter's sake!" Craig answered.

Lindsey shot me a "shut your mouth" look. I got up and went into the kitchen. I couldn't help feeling like something wasn't right. When I went back into the living room Craig and Summer were gone.

"Do you think something is up with those two?" I asked Lindsey.

"Summer is not stupid. Craig pays her bills. And he's smart enough to know that he is not someone that she would stay with, he is nothing like Carlos."

Lindsey and I had met Carlos, Summer's son's father. He was way different then Craig, more like the military gentleman type. Craig tries too hard to win Summer over. I hope she isn't going to get wrapped up with him because his wife was murdered. Never knowing anyone who had a family member murdered before made me feel so sick. I ran into the bathroom. As the water was running I thought about how horrible a person has to be to take another person's life; just another thing to shake my faith. I was already having doubts about religion and God and couldn't understand why God would let a child be hurt and abused? Why God would take away my Grandmother, the only person who cared about me. Why would God let his people feel so alone? Why would God let there be murder? That innocent child now has no mother.

At work the next night regulars who knew Craig were asking how he was and if he needed anything. Roxanne and I had been booked for a private party at a hotel on Market Street so I wasn't at the club long. I had to get some things from my locker for the private show. When I got to the hotel there were two judges, a city councilman, and two business types. I knew the one judge right away because I had just gone before him for a speeding ticket. He dropped the points but I still had to pay the fine. That was okay because I would make it back from him in his tips tonight (he-he). The gentlemen were seated at a table in the suite. They had started a poker game and were smoking cigars and drinking. If it was one thing I couldn't stand it was cigar smoke. Yuk! Roxanne was just finishing up her routine, said 'Hello' to me, and then headed into the adjoining room with Jack, one of the businessmen. He was a regular client of hers. Something was up, there was a Jacuzzi running and they shut the door.

It's better that way. I didn't want to know what was going on. Besides, I was too busy busting the judges chops because he didn't let me out of my ticket completely. He was so embarrassed, it was pretty funny. After my routine was finished one of the judges and I went back to Delilah's. Lindsey was there. She started to hang on the judge I brought back with me. In fact, she was all over him. He was divorced so that was okay. She pulled me along to join them on his boat. It was docked off of Delaware Avenue the coat was bright white and the water was dark. There were other boats out but I was still scared. Lindsey kept begging to drive the boat. NO WAY! But the judge let her drive. The judge strategically placed himself behind Lindsey and "guided her" along the way. I saw his hands up her skirt. All of a sudden we were doing like 90 miles an hour. I felt like my face was being pulled off and wasn't having fun anymore. My nails left tear marks in the judge's leather seats. I wanted to get off the boat. The judge slowed the boat down and we glided to shore. I got off and called to Lindsey. She wasn't coming with me. I reached out to her and she pushed my hand away. I couldn't believe it. Screw her then. I hope they don't find her floating in the river tomorrow morning.

I caught a taxi back to Delilah's, got in my car and went home. Lindsey pissed me off. I knew she was going through something but you don't act like that. I'm lonely too, with three years left before I'm done with college. I can't afford my own place. I pass these huge homes every day before getting to the townhouses I live in and ask myself, Who the hell lives there? I can't help but wonder what am I doing wrong?

I couldn't sleep when I got home. I opened a bottle of wine and sat out on the deck. There was a guy across the way on his patio having a beer. I waved and he waved back. He asked me if I wanted to come down and hang out. I figured why not?

"Hi, my name is Jim; I am a realtor in Newtown. I've seen you out on the deck at night having a drink and was going to ask you to join me before, but I thought you would say no."

"Well, I guess you never know until you try, I'm Amanda and I go to the community college in Newtown. Do you want to have sex?" Jim dropped his glass.

"Where did that come from? I mean, yes, it sounds great. You just surprised me."

It wasn't about surprise. I think it was my utter frustration that had the best of me. He was so shy.

"You can touch me anywhere you want."

He fumbled with my belt. I took my shirt off and held my boobs in my hands.

"Do you like these?"

"Uh, huh"...Jim reached out to touch them.

"Come on, I want you to fuck the shit out of me."

Jim finally came alive. He had me up against the wall and kissed real hard, picked me up, and put me on top of his dresser. He went down and made me so wet; then carried me over to his bed. Thank God he has a big penis! I was worried because he's a short man. I let him get on top. I didn't want to take complete control. To make things worse I fell asleep at his place. I woke up and Jim was cooking breakfast. What have I done? I needed to get the hell out of there. I was getting sucked in for breakfast. Maybe it is the least I can do. I smiled and sat down at the breakfast bar. He was happy. I opened the paper. There were still no suspects in the murder of Craig's wife. It was so sad. Jim asked me what I did for a living. I told him I was a full time student living off of the money my grandparents left me. He seemed intrigued and started to ask me about finances and if I had any investments.

"Look at the time! I have to run."

Jim kissed me goodbye. I suddenly didn't find him attractive anymore, grabbed my things and walked out the door. He stopped me and asked when he could see me again.

"You know where I live, stop by."

I came home and Lindsey was asleep on the couch. There was a message on the machine from Summer. She wanted to go shopping. I showered and headed back out, stopping to make sure Lindsey was breathing and she was. I covered her with a blanket. She was a bitch sometimes but I loved her.

When I got to my car there was a single red rose underneath my windshield wiper. There was a note wrapped around it. It said,

'Thanks for the awesome night, can't wait to see you again.... J.'

How did he know what kind of car I drove? STALKER! Summer and I went to Cherry Hill Mall. They had some good stores. The Express store was huge. I loved White House Black Market and just wanted to forget everything for a while and shop like I had money. I think Summer felt the same except she wasn't shopping as extensively as she normally did.

"What's wrong?' I asked.

"Nothing, I'm alright. My tips just weren't so hot this week."

"Are you okay? Do you need cash?"

"No, Amanda, I'm fine. I just have to watch my money right now."

"Is it because Craig hasn't been at the club all week? Have you heard from him?"

"Yes, he called last night. He said the cops were at his house all day yesterday and that they took boxes of things. He told me if the police contact me I am suppose to say I don't know him."

"Summer, are you and Craig going to get together now?"

"Oh no, we're just friends. He asks for more all of the time but he knows where I stand."

"So do the cops think he killed her?"

"I don't know what they think; I just keep watching the news for updates like everyone else."

We went to Olive Garden and had Sangria at the bar.

"So, you will never guess what or should I say who I did last night. Do you know the suit and tie guy who lives diagonal from us at the townhouse?"

"The one who drives the Lexus and plays with the remote control car in the parking lot?" asked Summer.

"Yes, that's him. We had crazy SEX last night!"

"What the hell is a matter with you? You NEVER have sex with the neighbors! It's like shitting where you lay. You idiot! Now you're going to end up with a peeping Tom."

"No way, you really think so?" we laughed.

I dropped Summer off at her apartment and went home to try and go to sleep. Lindsey came into my room.

"Alright, who the hell is Jim, why is he keeping me awake all day?"

"Are you kidding?" I asked.

"Do I look like I am freaking kidding?"

So, I told Lindsey the story.

"You, ass! He's going to drive us nuts now! Didn't your mother ever tell you not to shit where you lay."

Why did that sound so familiar? Lindsey went back out to the living room and put a pillow over her head. Then the doorbell rang.

"Amanda, it's for you!" Lindsey shouted. She walked by me and whispered,

"You better fix this!"

I came down the stairs and it was Jim. I said "hi" and then asked him to go for a walk with me.

"Look about last night. I'm not looking for a relationship right now."

"Please just give me a chance. I'm a good guy. Can we just start over and go out on a real date?"

"It is not you. Really it's me. I'm at a crossroad in my life."

Guys do this all of the time. Why did I feel so bad? Maybe I have a conscious? As I was walking up the steps I heard Lindsey chanting:

"Stalker, Stalker."

"You shut up. You still aren't off the hook for the other night!"

"Come on, it wasn't me it was the alcohol. I've been through a lot lately. I just wanted to drown my sorrows. I didn't mean to hurt you."

I went into my kitchen to pour a glass of wine and there was Jim, sitting on his patio. I hope he didn't think I was going out there. Boy, did I learn my lesson.

Lindsey and I were going to drive to work together the next morning. The club was opening at noon. I slept like a rock that night and must have needed it. I unwillingly dragged myself out of bed and into the shower. I was in a decent mood. Lindsey came in while I was getting ready. She had a great idea, IHOP for breakfast. Eggs Benedict is my favorite. It is so bad for you but it tastes so good. I threw my things into my bag and locked the front door, turned around, and Lindsey was coming toward me with this horrified look on her face.

"What's up?" I asked.

"I don't know how to tell you this."

She didn't have to say anything because I saw it for myself.

My windshield was smashed, my antenna was broken off and my car was keyed all of the way around.

"Who the hell would do this?" I asked.

"I'll give you one guess, he lives right there! I told you he was a psycho! You don't listen to me when I talk."

I called my cop friend Kevin. He was coming off duty from the following night and came over with another local cop. Kevin walked up to me and said,

"So, who did you piss off? Apparently it was someone with a temper."

Jim came out his door and picked up his newspaper. He said, "Looks like your day isn't starting out so well, Amanda."

Kevin chimed in real quick.

"What is that suppose to mean? I think you and I need to have a little talk."

Lindsey belted out that he was probably the one that did it. I went back into the house and got a tarp to cover my car. Kevin came back over without Jim.

"I don't know what you did to that guy but stay away from him. He's out to get you and wants to file a harassment complaint against you. He probably did damage your car, but there's no way we can charge him without a witness."

"Are you kidding me? That guy trashes my car and he is going to get away with it. And he wants to file a complaint against me??? I can't believe this is happening?"

"Come on, I will give you a ride to work."

"Sorry about breakfast, Lindsey."

"No big loss, I had more fun watching Jim squirm." Kevin hung out at the club. There was some big game on he wanted to watch. I was working the bar today and Kevin knew I would hook him up. I went into the locker room and put my things away. Lindsey came around the corner and said,

"So, why aren't you and Kevin together? It's so obvious that he has a thing for you."

"Girl, you need to mind your business."

"All I am saying is that he's cute and someone is going to snatch him up if you don't" snapped Lindsey.

Whatever, I went out to the bar and started setting up. My manager, Mike, came around and told me I needed to loosen another button on my blouse. I just rolled my eyes. He turned around and I smiled. I heard a woman's voice behind me say,

"Coors light bottle." It was Summer.

"Hey girl, what are you doing here?" I asked.

I popped the top on her bottle and handed it to her. She looked sad. It was starting to get busy so I really couldn't chat but told her to hang out and I would spend time with her during my break. Then I heard,

"We apologize for the interruption, we have breaking news. There has been a new development in the death of a lower Merion woman."

It clicked then; Summer knew something was up. I looked at her and she mouthed the words,

"He did it."

"Shut up" I told her.

I had my boss cover the bar while I took Summer outside.

"Craig killed his wife" said Summer.

"What the hell, why?" I asked.

"He did it for the insurance money. He stole from a lot of people; he did a lot of bad things."

"Holy shit, so what happens now?" I asked.

"Craig is going to confess tomorrow. I have to get the hell out of here."

"Come home with me tonight and we could face this thing together."

"Just don't tell anyone what I have told you."

Summer was going home to gather some things.

"I will be back to pick you up at the end of your shift" I offered, and went back into the club when Kevin passed me.

"Hey, do you need a ride home?"

"No, I answered. Summer is going to drive me." Kevin looked disappointed. I pulled him into a corner, put his hands on my hips and kissed him right on the mouth! I think he was shocked at first. Then, he tightened the grip on my hips and kissed me back. I released myself and went back over to the bar. He followed me and said,

"You want to tell me what that was all about?"

"I don't know what you're talking about. I have to get back to work. You're going to get me in trouble."

I raised my eyebrows and looked over at my boss. You see, the club had a rule. No boyfriends allowed in the club while you are working. I guess they do that so these men don't flip out if someone paws their woman. It makes sense. Kevin said,

"I get it, but this conversation is far from over."

"Amanda" I heard someone call my name.

I looked up and it was Roxanne's regular customer Jack.

"Is Roxanne in today?" he asked.

"I haven't seen her, but that doesn't mean she's not in later. Go check the board."

Jack threw a $5 in my tip jar and walked away. He was weird. The bar was slowing down. I started wiping the counters down and cleaning the glasses. Kevin came back up to the bar.

"So, are you ready to tell me what that kiss was all about?" he asked.

"It was just a thank you kiss for helping me with my car," I answered.

"No, No, No", you're lying!"

I sent him away and said "call me later". That seemed to satisfy him for the time being. Kevin left and I had to get ready to do my set. I really needed the money right now. I had no idea how much it was going to cost to fix my car. I had a red mini on with white thigh high boots and did a pole routine to ZZ tops She's Got Legs. There were some biker dudes dancing along. I couldn't remember the last time my ass was smacked so much. People crack me up. I walked the floor and collected my tips. Summer had just come in to pick me up, perfect timing. I gathered all of my stuff and we were out the door. The ride home down I-95 was gray and rainy. Lindsey was taunting me about Kevin from the back seat. Summer would just smile, when usually she would laugh. I knew there was a lot on her mind. We stopped to picked up Chinese food and some rental movies. We got back to the house and I started up the fireplace. I had to page through the phonebook to find someone to fix my car. Lindsey had no idea about what was going on with Summer. Just as we sat down to eat there was a news break on TV. The reporter said

"We have information that someone is turning themselves in at 9am tomorrow in connection with the death of Stefanie Rabinowitz. We will keep you updated when we have more information."

"So, did they catch the guy who killed Craig's wife?" Lindsey asked.

Summer burst into tears and began to tell Lindsey about Craig's confession to her. Craig told Summer he had taken his wife out to dinner and crushed Ambien in her wine to make her sleepy. Then, when they got home his wife, got into the bath and started to doze off. Craig said it was easy to hold her under the water while she drowned. Craig wasn't stupid. He was only coming out because he lost his battle for no autopsy. Craig was Jewish and was trying to stop the autopsy for religious reasons. Really they were selfish reasons. Craig didn't want to get caught. For the first time in her life Lindsey had nothing to say.

I gave Summer a glass of wine and a Xanax and told her it would help calm her down. Shit, my mom use to pop them like candy. I leaned into her and put my head on her shoulder.

"It will be alright" I told her.

I knew tomorrow was going to be hell for her. You can only be so strong. I put in the movie and we sat in silence.

I woke up the next morning with such a pain in the right side of my mouth. I went into the bathroom to rinse with some water. As soon as the cold water entered my mouth I thought I was going to hit the roof. The pain shot up the right side of my face. I felt around my mouth with my tongue and realized my tooth was broken in half; hope I didn't swallow it. If there was one thing I always took care of it was my teeth. I called my dentist and he couldn't see me until 2pm. That was fine. It gave me enough time to take a shower and pack a bag for work. Summer must have heard me on the phone because she rolled over and asked me what was wrong? I told her my tooth is broken and that we have to take a detour to my dentist's office before work. She didn't care. We turned on the news and there was Craig. They had him handcuffed as he was being escorted into the courthouse. The reporter was interviewing a family friend of the Rabinowitz's. The friend said that the whole family was shocked. That they could not believe that he would do something like this. This is the guy who was everybody's best friend. The reporter also said no motive had been released as of yet. Oh no, I thought, they are going to find all of the money Craig spent on Summer when they investigate. Maybe his wife found out money was missing and confronted him? Maybe that is why he killed her? Summer seemed relieved that her name wasn't mentioned. We turned off the news and got ready to go. Summer was nice enough to drive me. My dentist was so cool. He squeezed me in and took me right back. I have gone to the same dentist for years. He knows I don't complain so he figured it really had to hurt. He took one look in my mouth and said

"Are you under a lot of stress?"

I just looked at him.

"I know, who isn't under stress these days? It looks like you have been grinding your teeth at night and that is probably what broke your tooth."

He put temporary filler in and sent me on my way. I made an appointment to come back in two days for all of the work he needed to do. I just needed the pain to stop. Summer and I stopped and got coffee. We figured traffic on I-95 may be bad so we wanted to be prepared. We actually made good time getting to Delilah's. We turned down the street the club was on and I noticed a bunch of news vans parked along the sides of the street.

Chapter Six

She Works Hard For The Money

My stomach became full of knots. The reporters were beating on Summer's car.

"Summer, what was your relationship with Craig Rabinowitz? Summer, is it true you have accepted over $100,000 from Mr. Rabinowitz? Summer, did you know Craig was going to kill his wife in order to finance his life with you?"

Summer panicked and parked her truck at Delilah's front door. She pulled her hoodie over her head and said

"Ready; one, two, three, run!"

We ran into the club.

"What the hell was that all about?" I asked.

Christy was sitting at the bar with the news on. She told us that the news was reporting that Craig killed his wife so he could be with Summer. The cops found an expense list in a shoe box at Craig's house. The list had Summer's picture paper clipped to it. The news was reporting that Summer was his motivation for murder. Craig's expense list was as follows:

CRAIG'S EXPENSE LIST
STEFANIE'S LIFE INSURANCE-$1,800,000
SALE OF HOUSE-$300,000
TOTAL- $2,100,000
MINUS DEBT- $671,000
CASH TO LIVE ON- $1,429,000

The first thing Summer did was call her ex who was caring for her son. Her voice changed when she spoke to Anthony speaking soft and very sweet. I could tell she was nervous. Summer told her ex to keep the TV off and she would explain later. I didn't know what to do for her and felt so bad. I couldn't imagine what was going through her mind.

The club was empty. I guess the reporters scared all of the married men away. Our boss came up to me.

"Hey Amanda, why don't you take Summer home? It looks like we will be okay here without you two."

Summer put her head down on the counter. I took the keys to her SUV and told her to wait for me out back. I stepped out of the club and was suddenly blinded by all of the flashes. Now I know what celebrities feel like with the paparazzi. The flashing stopped when they realized I wasn't Summer. I told the reporters to leave me alone and said that I was just moving her car. The tires screeched as I turned the corner. Summer jumped into the backseat.

"Stay down." I told her.

We drove through a back alley and came out on a side street tricking the reporters. We stopped at Summer's apartment so she could get some things, driving by first to make sure the place wasn't staked out. Whew! It was safe. She ran in and ran out. Her cell started to ring. It was Craig. Summer threw her phone out the car window.

"I can't take anymore," cried Summer.

"It will be okay." I told her.

We went back to the house to devise a plan. Lindsey was home and in a bitchy mood.

"You know Summer, this is all your fault! You should've known better. You took advantage of him and fed into his need to have sex with you. What did you say? Did you ask him for more money?" Lindsey asked.

"You don't know what you're talking about! You of all people are going to play a martyr? Like you never asked a customer for a few more bucks."

"Knock it off; you're both being ridiculous. No matter what happened, Summer is our friend and we have to protect her."

I am not sure what Lindsey's problem was. Maybe Lindsey was jealous of all the nice things Summer had because of Craig. Maybe she was just being miserable.

The house phone rang. It was the club manager, Mike.

"Hey, I have a detective here looking for Summer. I'm going to put him on."

The cop got on the phone and said he needed to speak with Shannon. I knew he meant business. Not many people knew Summer's real name. The detective said that he was willing to come to us. I put him on hold.

"Alright Summer, are you ready to deal with this? I asked.

"Tell him to come here; I would love to get this over with."

I gave the detective directions. He said he was on the way.

In the meantime, we made sure we had all of our ducks in a row. Luckily enough, Summer, Lindsey, and I were together the night Craig's wife was killed. I knew she didn't have anything to do with the murder. She's not the type and doesn't have the stomach for it. The doorbell rang. It was the detective. He introduced himself and said he was here to conduct an investigation into the death of Stefanie Rabinowitz. He interviewed us all individually. No moral support was aloud. The detective asked me a lot of questions: What is your full name? Where do you reside? How long have you known the exotic dancer known as Summer? How long have you known Craig

Rabinowitz? What was the nature of their relationship? Where were you the night Stefanie Rabinowitz was murdered?

Thank God that was over. Two hours later he concluded his investigation and left. I was so stressed out. I needed a warm bubble bath, went into the bathroom and started the tub running. The house was quiet. Lindsey went to her room and Summer was lying on the living room couch. Just as I added bubbles and lit my lavender candles the phone rang. It was Kevin. He saw Summer on the news. I told him I did not want to involve him with what was going on and told him that at this point, the less you know the better. Especially, since he was a cop.

"The cops interviewed me today. They asked basic questions. He only asked me to go into detail on a few things."

"Well, from the sound of it you should be okay." "Should" being the operative word.

"So, what are you doing now?" Kevin asked.

"I am filling the tub? Why?"

"Um, because I am in the driveway! '

"Oh, then I'll be right down to get you."

I grabbed a towel and ran down the steps. Kevin was already at the door. He followed me in and chased me back to the bathroom. I told him to wait right there while I went to the kitchen. I poured two glasses of wine and grabbed a bowl of grapes from the fridge. Kevin was already submerged in the tub when I got there. I handed him his wine and joined him in the bath. I turned around so he could wash my back for me. It felt so good. There was a sexual tension between us. I knew he was pissed when he found out I slept with the neighbor but he never said a word. Kevin was that kind of guy; if I could only put him in a bottle and save him for a few more years. I wasn't ready for a serious relationship. I knew he was someone I could fall in love with if I let myself. Kevin was such a gentleman. He didn't even make a move. We talked more about Summer and Craig.

"So, tell me did they sleep together?"Kevin wasn't stupid.

"Will you believe me if I tell you no?" I asked.

"There is no way they did not sleep together. There was over $100,000 involved between the two of them. I don't think he was just being a good friend."

Kevin was right. I just didn't want to believe that someone would manipulate someone else for their benefit. I have too much of a conscious. I could never pull it off. Kevin and I soaked for a little longer.

"I just rented a few movies. Do you want to stay and watch something?" I asked.

"I don't see why not. I have no other plans."

We got out of the tub and dried off. I put a cute pair of pajamas on. Kevin jumped in my bed and covered himself with blankets and pillows. He was so silly. I put the movie in and lied down next to him. I was so relaxed I must have drifted off to sleep.

My alarm clock was going off. Kevin was sleeping next to me. I stroked his arm and whispered into his ear,

"Did I fall asleep?"

"Yes, you did" he said.

"I have to go to school. But if you want to hang out here we can have lunch when I get back."

I guess he thought that was a plan because he rolled back over.

I took Summer's car to school and grabbed the paper out of the door before leaving. I was glad I did because there was more about Summer in it. I read the article on the way to class. As soon as I sat down my mind began to wander. I had flashbacks of Kevin sleeping. He looked so serene. Who would have thought a cop would go for a stripper? That's kind of funny. What would he tell his mom that I did for a living? Maybe he would tell her I was independently wealthy? I tuned back in to hear the teacher saying something about humans as social beings. We all thrive on interactions and advice from one another. Man, did she hit the nail on the head. That was it, class was over. How did I lose 50 minutes? It is not like I don't have anything on my mind. I practically skipped all of the way to the car. I got home and Kevin wasn't there. I was disappointed. It was the first time I got sick before I ate. It was probably the let down. I was looking forward to spending time with Kevin. This is exactly why I don't let people in. I can't stand it when my feelings get hurt. I went into the kitchen and started pulling things out of the fridge for lunch. There was a note from Lindsey on the counter. She took Summer over to see her son. I hoped that helped her feel better. The front door opened and Kevin came in.

"What are you doing? I thought we were going out to lunch?"

"I was kind of ticked off when I came home and saw you were not here. I decided to make something to eat."

"Well put it in the fridge and save it for later. We're still going out." Then he pulled flowers out from behind his back." Surprise! I didn't stay here was because I didn't want Lindsey and Summer to see me. I figured I had to go out and get you something."

I think the last time I got flowers was my senior prom. I clipped the ends from the flowers and put them in some water.

"So, said Kevin, where do you want to go for lunch?"

"Let's go to Old City! We can take a walk around and enjoy the weather. We could have lunch at The Plow and the Stars. That place is beautiful, so classic inside.

"Alright, Old City it is!"

I think Kevin would have gone to the moon if I asked. The drive downtown was smooth. We didn't hit any traffic. That is always nice. I was surprised the restaurant was packed for lunch. We sat at a table by the window, my favorite place to sit. I loved people watching. I also loved the food there. The garlic bread they served with my chicken Cesar salad was excellent. Kevin ordered a portabella mushroom steak. It looked so good but I was trying to watch my weight. My cell rang. It was Summer.

"Hey, have any plans for tonight?"

"No, Not really, why?"

"Do you feel like going to the fair tonight with me and Anthony? I really need to go some place where no one will recognize me."

I knew she needed some down time and told her to hold on for one minute. I asked Kevin if he would come with us in case we were bothered by anyone. He said he was cool with that.

"Okay, Summer. That sounds like a plan. Meet me at my house around 6pm."

"So, how would you feel about us dating?"

I looked down and dug into my salad.

"Look, Kev; I do care about you but I'm not looking for a relationship right now."

Kevin cringed.

"We won't know if it will work unless we try?"

"I have to warn you, I am not girlfriend material; but if you really want to try, I will. Well, Craig's preliminary trial is tomorrow. I am going with Summer for moral support in case she is called to testify about her relationship with Craig."

"You are such a good friend to her and I don't understand why."

"Summer is not a bad person; she's just made some bad choices."

"I have to work tomorrow otherwise I would offer to go with you two."

"That's okay, besides I worry about your career. You're a cop; I don't want your career hurt because you get caught in a photograph with Summer."

"You're sweet but I wouldn't be there for Summer. Someone has to worry about you. I admire you standing by your friend and everything but people at my precinct are saying that Summer had Craig wrapped around her finger. They also think that she was stringing him along with promises of a marriage."

"I personally never heard a conversation like that between Summer and Craig. In fact, I only saw them together a few times outside of work. Craig never really spoke to me. Summer knows how expensive it is to raise children. I would hate to think she took all of that money from him knowing that he had a child who could have benefited from the funds."

Kevin paid the check and we went for a stroll. I loved Old City but could never afford to live in it. Kev reached out and took my hand. We walked close to each other. I had a brilliant idea,

"Let's go get my belly button pierced!"

"Really?" said Kevin.

It was something I had wanted to do for a while. So we found a place on South Street that did body piercing. I picked out a silver hoop with a purple stone dangling from it. Purple is my favorite color. Kev paid for it. I told him he didn't have to but he said he wanted to. Kev held my hand and laughed as I laid down in the chair. They made me sign some form saying that if it gets infected and I get sick I couldn't sue them. How hard could it be to take care of? Besides, I would die if some nasty stuff ever started to come out of it. The guy doing the piercing wasn't real friendly. He took some cold brown stuff and rubbed it on my belly button. Then he said,

"Ready; 1, 2, 3!"

I felt a sting and it was over. It wasn't so bad. I stood up and looked in the mirror. I couldn't believe I actually did it. I caught a glimpse of the time. It was getting late. I wanted to get on Interstate 95 before rush hour traffic.

We got home in time for me to change for the fair. Kevin sat on the bed as I threw clothes all over deciding what to wear.

"We're going to a fair, right? Not a runway show" he asked.

I pushed him back on the bed and wrapped a bra around his wrists. Kev freed his hands and wrapped them around my waist. He rolled me over, I pulled his shirt off and we started to kiss. It got wild. I broke out the orange sherbet massage oil. I pulled his pants down and rubbed lube all over his dick. Forget what Lindsey said about licking it like an ice cream cone. He was more like my banana split. His dick even bent a little like a banana. All the better to hit my G spot with. I licked and sucked on every spot I could. He squealed with delight. I couldn't believe how into me he was. He kept touching my face and telling me how beautiful I was. He kissed me gently, and we got it on so slow. The sex was incredible. He made me come so hard I thought I was going to hit the ceiling. He followed me into the shower. I turned it into a sauna.

"You're going to burn my skin off!" screamed Kevin.

"Oh my God; there is nothing better than a steaming hot shower."

Just then I heard Summer come in with Anthony. I'm glad I locked my bedroom door. We got dressed. Kevin walked out first. Summer started to laugh.

"So, it finally happened," she laughed.

Kev broke into tune. He was singing something about searching for a real love. What a big dork!

Anthony was so excited. He couldn't wait to get to the fair. I loved the fair too. Who doesn't? The fair is such a happy place with popcorn, candy, games and rides. There is nothing else like it. I loved the smells and the cool, night air. Summer walked ahead with Anthony. Kev grabbed my hand. A fellow officer came up that knew him. I couldn't wait to hear how Kevin was going to introduce me." Rich, this is my girlfriend Amanda," he said. Ha! Girlfriend! Kev introduced me to

Rich's wife Amy. She was a snob. She acted like they had no time for us. I turned and went the other way. Summer was taking Anthony on the kiddy rides. Kev and I played some games and grabbed a slice of pizza. We met up with Summer and Anthony at the Win a Fish game. You had to get a ping pong ball into a glass bottle and you would win a goldfish. Kevin picked Anthony up and they got a bucket of ping pong balls. After throwing twenty ping pong balls the boys walked away with two goldfish. I think we were all ready for bed. Tomorrow was going to be a tough day.

Summer dropped us off at the townhouse. Kevin said he wanted to stay. That was fine but I was *really* just going to bed. We both had to leave at the same time the next morning anyway. Kevin had to be at work by 9am and that is when we had to be in court by. I went to the kitchen to get a glass of wine.

"Why do you drink so much wine?" Kevin asked.

"It helps me relax." I answered.

"Did you ever think about finding something else beside wine to relax you?"

"No, I didn't think I had to. Besides, wine is good for you." I don't think I liked his line of questioning. What is the big deal? I fell asleep without drinking it anyway.

Chapter Seven

Judgement Day

Kevin woke me up in time to get ready for court. He was leaving to go home and get ready. He didn't have any clean work uniforms with him. The phone rang. It was Summer.

"Listen, can you just meet me at the courthouse?"

"It is a little short notice Sum. I still don't have a car. I'll have to wake up Lindsey and see if I can borrow hers. Why, what is going on?"

"I'm running behind and still have to drop the baby off at the sitters. I'm afraid I won't have enough time to pick you up."

Lindsey said taking her car was fine. I got ready and left. I started to get nervous, had a sharp pain in my stomach, need to use the bathroom. I just couldn't believe what has happened. Could obsession really drive a man to commit murder? How could Craig kill the mother of his child? What kind of monster would do such a thing? Well, I guess we were about to find out. I got to the courthouse with time to spare. There were news vans everywhere. I called Summer on my cell to find out where she was. Apparently, she was already there and asked me to meet her in the corridor of the parking garage that leads to the courthouse. I pulled into the garage Summer was right there. She looked frazzled. That wasn't like her.

"What's going on?" I asked.

She had gone to the jail before coming to the courthouse to speak with Craig.

"Are you crazy? What were you thinking?"

"I led him on Amanda. I kept asking for more and more money and he would give it to me. I told him that if he couldn't produce the money I would cut all contact with him." said Summer. I freaked out on her.

"You may have led him on, but you didn't make him kill his wife. Look, this isn't the time to break down. Right now we need to walk in there cool and collected. Her family is in there and I am sure they hate you. Everyone is going to hang on your every word and action." I pulled her into the corner and wiped her eyes." Take a deep breath, here we go." I took her arm in mine and we walked into the courtroom.

People's heads spun around like the exorcist. The courtroom became quiet. It was like walking into homeroom that fateful day years ago. Then the whispers began. It was Déjà Vu.

"Order in the court!" called the court officer.

Craig was being escorted in by prison guards. We sat down and everything was silent.

"On the murder of Stefanie Rabinowitz, how do you plead?"

"Guilty, Your Honor."

"On the charge of theft by deception, how do you plead?"

"Guilty, Your Honor."

"On the charge of deceptive business practices, how do you plead?"

"Guilty, Your Honor."

There were gasps in the courtroom. I guess we all had assumed there would be a trial. We weren't expecting a guilty plea. The judge asked Craig if he would like to make a statement. Craig did. I couldn't wait to hear this:

"I made the decision based on what I believe to be the most important factors. Number one is my guilt. That I am guilty of these charges and I am ready to accept full responsibility for my wife Stefanie's death. I cannot and will not subject my daughter, Haley, my wife's family, my mother-in-law and my brother-in-law, my family and our friends to what most assuredly would be a very painful trial and one that I am sure would bring much sadness and anguish to all of those involved. I have brought enough heartache and devastation to all of these people and so many others as well. I decided to change my plea when three of my dead loved ones – my wife, my father-in-law and my father visited me in a dream Tuesday night. They said Craig, sit down; we have to talk to you. They put their hands on my hand and said, Craig, it's time for you to do what is right. It is time for you to do the right thing," he finished.

The Assistant District Attorney said evidence showed Craig slipped sleeping medicine into his wife's drink so she could not defend herself against his attack. Then he choked the life out of her. The autopsy showed that Mrs. Rabinowitz died at least two hours before her husband called the police. That news devastated me. By Craig pleading guilty, the death penalty was taken off of the table. Craig was sentenced to life behind bars. I grabbed Summer by the arm and pulled her out of the courthouse. The cameras were flashing as we left. Thank God that was over! I could tell Summer was upset. As we walked people were calling her names like "slut", "bitch" and "whore". The whole situation was tragic.

Summer wanted to go home and sleep and I had to get Lindsey's car back to her. I told Summer to come over later and we will all go out. We needed to move on with our lives. I called Kevin to see how his day was going.

"You will never guess what happened at court."

"I already heard. It's all over the news. What are you doing tonight?"

"If you don't mind, I think I'll hang out with the girls."

"No that is fine. I'm going to work a double anyway so I'll see you tomorrow."

"Hey Lindsey, do you want to go out tonight?" I asked.

"Yes. Roxanne asked if we wanted to do something tonight. I'll call her. I'm sure she'll be in."

The more the merrier I always say! Everyone met at our house at 7pm. I looked cute with black dress pants and a burgundy, lacy button down shirt. We decided to go to a club on Delaware Avenue called the 8th Floor. It was a nice place. There were French doors leading outside. The roof had lights strung along the perimeter. We found a table outside and ordered drinks. It wasn't long before we were comfortable. There were way more men than women at the club. The competition was fierce. I don't think I paid for a drink all night. It's all good. We were laughing and dancing. I was really enjoying myself. Summer and Lindsey had already found a man to cuddle with. That left Roxanne and I at the table.

"So, do you go to school?" I asked.

"Yes. I go to the community college in Newtown."

"Really? That is the same college I go to. What's your major?"

"I'm not sure. I like drama and I like music. I was thinking about music therapy."

"That's cool. I'm majoring in nursing. My Grandmother lost her mind when she was in her early 60s. I spent a lot of time with her and figured nursing was the next best thing. I could help take care of others."

"I know what you mean. My mom died when I was young. That was hard. I get along with my dad, but he is remarried now. I don't know how I feel about that. I dance to pay my college tuition and it helped me develop acting skills as well" she giggled seeming like a good kid.

I wanted to check out the view from the roof so I took a walk over.
A quick guy in a suit caught Roxanne's attention. Good for her. Just
then I was overwhelmed by cheap cologne. I looked up and this man
sat down at my table. His hair looked soaking wet, he obviously used
fake tanner and when he smiled I was blinded by the light. Holy bleach
use tooth man.

"Hey, my name is Todd. What's your name?"

"My name is Amanda," I responded politely.

"Do you have a boyfriend Amanda?"

But before I could answer there was a kiss on the back of my neck.
I turned around and it was Bob. Remember fast Bob, from the club?
I was pleasantly surprised. You could say he saved me. When I turned
back around Todd was gone.

"Did I interrupt?" asked Bob.

"No, not at all. Actually, I would have enjoyed myself more if
someone stabbed me in the eye."

Bob laughed. "Glad I could be of assistance."

"Are you following me?" I asked.

"Why yes. I planted a GPS on your G-string."

"Smart ass!

You never called" he commented.

"I know, I've been busy."

"Well, what are you doing now?" he asked.

"Sitting here, talking to you."

"Come on, let's dance."

Bob pulled me out onto the dance floor. He smelled like expensive cologne and weed. That's what Bob was good for – weed supply. When we were young he smoked it every night. He said it helped him fall asleep. See, I knew my combination of wine and vomiting wasn't such a bad routine. Bob was the tall, dark and handsome type. His family had old money. Fast Bob drove a new black convertible mustang and worked at his dad's auto shop. He couldn't wait to take the business over. He was hot and he knew it. That is why I would never date him afraid of the feelings I got when with him. I lost my self control. Bob started to kiss me and I couldn't help but to kiss him back. It got pretty hot. He found that spot behind my ear. The situation was becoming dangerous. I heard Lindsey say

"Get a room!"

Thank God my friends had re-grouped. I had to get out from under Bob's spell. I was ready to go home before I got myself into more trouble.

Sitting at in the back on the way home was a smart place to be because Lindsey was driving like a freaking nut! We were going the wrong way on Interstate 95! I screamed for her to stop the car. Lindsey crossed the barrier and turned around. I thought I was going to die and she was laughing. It sounded like the muffler fell off of the car. I was physically and emotionally exhausted. I had just gotten comfortable in bed when Kevin came in. I pretended to be asleep feeling guilty about kissing Bob. Kevin was ranting and raving that it smelled like a bar in here. I didn't even acknowledge him. If there is one thing I have learned it is that you need to pick your battles. Kevin finally just laid down and went to sleep. Thank God!

I woke up before Kevin the next morning, put the teapot on, and went outside to get the paper. There was a guy with a tow truck hooking up to Lindsey's car.

"Can I help you?"

"No, thanks I got what I came for. This car is being repossessed for failure to make payments."

I ran into the house and pulled Lindsey out of bed and then sent Kevin out front with her to try to talk to the guy. They had no luck and the man left with her car. Lindsey kept insisting she was only two payments behind. I think you have to be a little more behind than that for them to take your car.

I sat down at the kitchen table with my tea. Chef Kevin was trying his hand at homemade Eggs Benedict. Good luck with that. I have tried and it never tastes as good as the diner. Lindsey came in looking serious. I told her if she needed money she should have come to me and I would have helped her out. She had something to say to me. This didn't sound good. Lindsey sat down at the table and said,

"You have two weeks to find a new place to live."

"What? Why?"

I nearly spilled my hot tea all over.

"I haven't been paying the rent. We got evicted." Kevin had to sit on me because I was going to kill her!

"I'm so sorry. I've had so much fun going out and spending money that I spent too much and spent money that wasn't even mine. I feel horrible. I'm going to move in with my mom temporarily. We can get another place in a few months."

I glared at Lindsey and said,

"How could you do this to me? We need to go out anyway. My car is finished and I want to pick it up before the collision shop closes."

Shaking; I was so angry I went in my room, threw on some sweats and I was out of there.

"How could she do this? I trusted her."

"Don't worry. I'll talk to my roommate. Maybe you could move in with us."

But, I didn't want to move in with Kevin. I buried my head in my hands. This isn't happening to me. Not again.

We got to the collision center just in time. I had to pay $800 to fix my car; that poor, old Camaro. It didn't deserve to be treated like that. Kevin followed me home. I got into the left hand turn lane and waited for the green arrow. Just as I started to turn a car came through

the intersection and slammed into the passenger side of my car. I was
hit so hard that my car spun around and the rear axle broke. The car
was literally sitting on the ground. I looked up and saw a wheel roll
by. Kevin was banging on the driver's side window. He opened the car
door and I got out. I felt dizzy. I sat down on the curb and pushed my
hair behind my ears. I had blood dripping down my face. My head had
starred the windshield. My poor car couldn't catch a break either. I
curse everything that comes close to me. My car is definitely totaled.
The punk kid that hit me got out of his car screaming,

"You jumped the light! It's your fault!"

There were too many witnesses that saw him go through the red
light. I thought Kevin was going to kill him. Then the stupid kid tried
to run. It didn't take long for the cops to get there. Probably because it
was a main intersection and the two vehicles involved were not drivable.
I called the collision center I had just left. The manager told me to stop
messing with him. When he realized I was telling the truth he said he
would be right there to get my car. An ambulance pulled up. I told them
I was fine but the paramedic said I would need stitches. I was having a
really bad day. My vision was blurry. I let the paramedics take me to the
emergency room. My head was really starting to hurt and I felt nauseous.
I had never been in an ambulance before. They made me sit on a stretcher
and they put seatbelts on me. It was weird looking out the back door and
seeing the things you have just passed. I didn't like facing backwards.

When I entered the emergency room everyone knew Kevin. I was so embarrassed by the attention. I had blood all over my hands. The physician was so nice. He looked too young to be a real doctor. He said

"I want you to have a cat scan of your head. I think it's only a concussion. But, I want to make sure."

One of the nurses at my bedside said

"If you're dating Kevin then we really need to examine your head."

She was funny. But it hurt when I laughed. The cop from the accident scene came in to tell me that the kid who hit me had no insurance. I figured that when he tried to run.

The ER technician took me to cat scan. It was like sliding back and forth in a big open tire. A few minutes later and it was done. When I got back to my cubicle in the emergency room there was a woman standing there I had not seen previously. She introduced herself as Mary. She was the manager of the emergency department.

"I have a part-time ER technician position open, I want to know if you would be interested? The nurse and the physician who are taking care of you said you were very sweet."

That was a compliment.

"But, I have no experience."

"We can train you" Mary replied.

Mary gave me her business card and told me to call her when I was up to it.

It took eight stitches to close the wound on the right side of my forehead. At least it was along my hairline. I started to cry. I think everything just hit me. I had nowhere to live, no car, with only enough savings to fix one of my problems. I could put a down payment on a car or put the money I have up as a security deposit. Kevin said he had to make a phone call. I was just waiting on my discharge paperwork. When he came back over he said,

"Listen, I just talked to my roommate and it will be fine if you move in."

I just looked at him.

"Also, a good friend of mine is the manager at a car dealer down the street from here and he said he can help us replace your car. Let's at least go take a look" Kevin said. I couldn't wait to get out of this hospital gown and back into my clothes. One of the nurses brought over a scrub top for me to wear because my shirt had blood all over it. It almost looked like a scene from a murder movie. I signed my discharge papers and we walked out to the parking lot.

"Can you just take me home? I really don't feel like dealing with a car salesman right now."

"Come on now Amanda, just let me help you with this. I don't understand why you are so resistant to trust me. It would make me feel better to fix at least one of your problems today."

How could I say no? By now Kevin had guilted me into going to the dealership. He introduced the salesman as his friend Austin who seemed nice. What is it with the slicked back hair? I just don't think that is attractive. Austin talked fast. He had three cars for me to pick from that he could sell me with no money down. The first car was a Hyundai Scoop. It was burgundy with gray interior, it had a sunroof and a CD player. It was cheap for being almost brand new but way too small. The second car was a dark blue Honda Civic. It was loaded and clean but was a little more than I wanted to spend. The third car and the one that I picked was a two year old Z24 Cavalier. It was perfect in size and price. The only problem was it had a 5 speed stick shift which I had never driven a five speed before. Kevin said,

"It really isn't that hard to drive. If you truly like the car I will teach you how to drive it."

My payments were going to be $218 per month. That made me a little nervous. The Camaro I had was 10 years old and it was paid for but this cavalier was so much nicer. It had chrome wheels and a big spoiler on the back. Not to mention a CD player and sunroof. My old Camaro had a cassette player and roll up windows. What a difference.

"So, why don't we go get something to eat while Austin does the paperwork?" Kevin asked.

"I'm kind of hungry and I have to go to work later. Maybe we better eat now." I answered.

Kevin and I went to a nearby diner to eat. They had Eggs Benedict so I was set.

"Kev, I just don't get it. I feel like I'm being punished for something. I try so hard to do good things and I just can't get ahead in life."

"Will you stop feeling sorry for yourself? We can and will get through this."

I wondered if he would feel that way if he found out I kissed Bob? I'm just going to put that out of my mind right now and enjoy my eggs.

"I can pick up some over time at work and I'll help you with your car payment." Kevin said.

"No, really you don't have to." I told him.

I really did not want to owe him anything if we ever broke up. Is it horrible that I think that way? It's just with everything I have been through I have learned that good things simply don't happen to me.

We went back and picked up the car. Kevin was right. It did make me feel a little better. NICE. We drove the car back to Kevin's house. He wanted me to meet his roommate. Walt was at the house with his girlfriend Nicole. Nicole was perfect. She was attractive and had just graduated nursing school. She still lived with her mom so she could save money while going through school. Walt and Nicole even had a little nest egg together. I was so jealous of them. I blamed my crappy life on my parents. If they were good parents maybe I could move home and save money. But, we all know that will never happen, unless hell has frozen over and pigs are flying.

Nicole said, "So, Kevin tells me that you are in nursing school. I can help you with your work if you need it. Besides, if you are living here we will be hanging out a lot."

Then I started to think - maybe I will put school on hold for a while until I get my living situation settled. I could stop dancing and get a comfortable day shift job. But what would I do with no education? And if I stop going to school will I ever go back? All I need is a roommate. Then I can afford to stay in school. Oh God, here comes that anxious feeling again. I'll check out the paper tomorrow. It will all work out. I told myself to stop. I needed to keep it together.

"Nicole, really that sounds great; Listen Kev, I have to run. I have to get to work."

I kissed Kevin good bye.

"I'll call you later" he said with a smile.

Believe it or not I couldn't wait to get to work that night. I needed to free my mind for a little while. Delilah's was packed when I got there. We had two bachelor parties and one private party scheduled. I made sure all of the back rooms were stocked.

"Hey you!" called Roxanne, as I walked in.

She seemed like she was in a good mood. Her regular Jack had booked her for one of the parties and had also bought a case of Dom for his room. That alone was a bonus for Roxanne. The customer who rents the room gets charged for everything missing from the private bar at the end of the night plus everything they order from me. Let me tell you there is some expensive liquor stocked. After I finished checking the party rooms, I stopped in the locker room to chat.

Everyone was asking what happened to my head. I must have told the story fifty times. I fixed my bangs so you couldn't really notice the stitches. Out of the corner of my eye I noticed a woman slip into the back of the locker room. I asked the other girls if they knew her. No one admitted to it. I approached the woman and asked her what she was doing here.

"I'm sorry. I should have introduced myself. My name is Missy. I am the house mom at Diva's International Gentlemen's Club in Levittown, PA. The club is under new ownership and they want fresh faces. There is a sign on bonus if you try the club out for one month. Here is all of the contact information."

Roxanne and I live closer to Diva's then Delilah's. That is one good thing.

"I'm outta here! This place is full of bad memories."

Missy gave us invite cards to pass out to our best customers. The party rooms were starting to fill. Bachelor parties were always crazy but I have seen the corporate guys go nuts too. The gents in Roxanne's room were out of control and on my nerves. I had to tell them that if they touched me one more time they were leaving. I wasn't in the mood for their crap. My head still hurt from earlier today; nothing like starring a windshield first thing in the morning. The men in this room were a little too feisty for me. I told Roxanne not to let the crowd man handle her. She knew to call for me if she needed help. I came back to the bar and sent one of our best bouncers to watch Roxanne's room. I made shot rounds on the floor between doing stock while talking to some of my regulars. I gave them invites to the new club I would probably be going to and told them it was just time for a change. I made stock rounds again and Roxanne's room was kicking ass. The bar bill was already $1500. Management made me run Jack's credit card to make sure he was good for the money. The card cleared so I re-stocked the room. Roxanne looked good. Her tip roll was huge! I smiled and waved to her as I left her room. She was dancing to the band Live. It was one of her favorite routines. The night went well. I had $440 at cash out time. I walked out to the parking lot and Summer was getting into her SUV.

"So, are you going to check the new place out?"

"Yes, probably on Monday" I told her.

"I'll call you so we can go together."

"Sure, sounds good."

I felt nauseous and walked in front of my car and started to vomit on the curb. I was exhausted from a long day. It was definitely time to head home.

Bright and early the next morning Roxanne called.

"Hey, would you like to join me for an afternoon of shopping?"

"I would love to go shopping, but I have to check out the paper first to see if there are any ads for residence sharing. I need to find a place to live."

"Well how about this; I'll come over and if you want to check some places out I'll go with you."

"That sounds like a plan." I answered.

Well, there were only 3 ads for residence sharing: The first was a retired gentleman looking for a roommate, that won't work. The second ad, maybe a possibility, was a local college student looking for a roommate. The apartment wasn't far from where I lived now and it is in my price range. The third was a woman who wanted to rent a room in her home. The room in the house wouldn't work. As I continued to read the ad she specified no late hours and no sleepovers. Ok, let's look at the one bedroom apartments. As I scrolled down the page it became very apparent that I couldn't afford to live where I am now alone. Roxanne lived in Bensalem. She suggested some nice places we could check out there. Maybe I will just do that. Lindsey came out of her room with some boxes.

"Amanda, I really am sorry about this whole thing."

"I'm over it Lindsey, just let it go."

I *was* still really mad but it's not worth fighting about. Kevin called to find out what my plans were for the day. I told him I was going shopping with Roxanne. I didn't want to hurt his feelings so I was not telling him about the apartment hunting. He would get really upset. I just didn't want to live with him or anyone for that matter. I needed to work on myself before I can be good for anyone else.

Roxanne pulled up and beeped the horn. I grabbed my purse and said goodbye to Lindsey.

"Hey girl, how did you end up doing at the club last night?" I asked Roxanne.

"You will never believe it, I walked out with $1500 cash!"

"I knew you would do well with that party. So, what do you think of that guy Jack?"

"He's hard to explain; he's like Jeckle and Hyde. If things are going his way, he is great. But if things are not how he wants, he can get nasty. This one time, we had a fight and he grabbed me by both my arms and shook me. I had to set him straight. I told him that he better never ever touch me again"

I called the college kid looking for a roommate and he said Roxanne and I could stop by. We went to meet him first. I figured I would check it out only because it was the closest place available from school. And it was close to I-95. Hopefully, I will love the place and my search will be over. The guy's name was Charlie. When I walked into the apartment you could definitely tell that it was a guy living there. The place wasn't neat and tidy. That would drive me crazy. I caught

Charlie checking out my boobs. He walked us into the bedroom that would be mine. It was plain and small and didn't have its own bathroom. Honestly, it smelled funny. Charlie said,

"I have a few people interested. But if you make a decision today the place could be yours. Why don't you take a minute and think about it. I sense we would be great roommates."

I was so not flattered! I wanted to get him a tissue to wipe the drool from his mouth.

"You know what; I'll call you and let you know." As we were leaving Charlie said

"If you don't want to take the apartment, maybe we could meet for drinks?"

"I am sorry, but I have a boyfriend. In fact, he is a local cop."

"Oh, no, I just remembered I accepted a deposit on the apartment last night."

How convenient. Roxanne and I rolled our eyes as we left. I could smell a con man from a mile away. We looked over my list of apartments to check out. Roxanne turned my list of seven into a list of three. She scratched the others off because of either area or clientele. I respected her honesty. The first place we checked out was on Street Road. It was fine for me. It even had a washer and dryer which was nice. There was a pool and the complex was nestled in a neighborhood. I didn't want to be on a busy road and enjoyed keeping a low profile when I could. That's why I loved where I lived. I filled out an application for those apartments. The only problem was they had two bedroom apartments available, but no one bedroom apartments right now. The extra $115 for a two bedroom could put me over budget. The next place we went to see were really nice townhouses by the local mall which were so spacious. It didn't feel like a rental complex. They were well manicured and some places had their own front yard plants and mini flags. It was at the top of my price range though. The final place we went to see was by the racetrack. Put it this way, we saw the people standing on the corner and we kept driving. I just got a ghetto feeling from the place. Also, it was too close to the racetrack. So I waited to see if I was approved. It sucked though just because I hardly had any credit didn't mean I was not going to pay my rent. But they didn't look at it that way. I guess I could understand. It's all about the money.

Roxanne and I had lunch at the mall. We shopped a little them went back to my house and took a little longer than planned as Roxanne had other things to do. Roxanne had just left when Kevin came in with empty boxes.

"We should get to packing. After all, you only have two weeks left here."

I started to panic. Two weeks and I had so much to do.

"Can we just relax tonight? I want to spend time together and do nothing."

Kev must have realized that I was stressed out. He brought me a bowl of ice cream and sat down next to me. I wished I could just stay here but that was out of the question. The landlord was going to put the townhouse up for sale.

"That's it!"

"That's what?" said Kevin.

"I'm going to apply for a mortgage and try to buy this townhouse. I'm going to call the landlord and see how much he's asking for it."

"Are you sure that is what you want to do? Because if it is I have a friend I can call that's a realtor."

I called the landlord. He wasn't a bad guy, he just wanted his rent. I told him about what I was thinking and he told me he was going to ask $104,000 for the townhouse. He said he would consider selling it to us for less if we paid the past two months rent and next month's rent so he knew we were for real. Kevin's real estate friend told us to come in the office on Monday and he would see if he could get me approved. I was excited. Maybe this is it. Maybe things were finally going to turn my way.

"Let's head to bed, my love. I need to show you how thankful I am for everything you are doing for us."

"Okay, but only if I can get to use the peppermint stuff on you!" he said.

We were both naked before we hit the sheets. I snuck in some spray whipped cream, sprayed it on his fingers, and then licked it off. I sprayed it on his nipples and licked it off. I sprayed it on his stomach, and licked it from there. I sprayed it on the head of his penis and licked it from there too! I couldn't help myself. I tossed the can and jumped on top of him. I sat him up and used the headboard to hold onto as I bounced up and down. Kev held on to my boobs, he loved watching them jiggle. That made me hot.

Chapter Eight
No One Else Will Do

The next morning Kevin and I were sitting at the kitchen table having coffee.

"So what are your plans today?" Kevin asked.

"I am going to meet the girls so we can check out that new club in Bristol," I answered.

"I thought we talked about this Amanda. I want you to give up dancing and take the hospital job."

I could tell he was unhappy.

"Eventually I would love to have that job, Kev. But right now I cannot live on $9. 00/hr."

"Listen to me; I'm due for a raise. I can help you get through school. This job will be a good experience for you."

I just looked at the floor. You can't talk to Kevin when he gets like this. He's very old fashioned at heart and won't admit it. I knew he wanted to be the bread winner. He meant well but I needed to do this for myself. I got ready and left to meet the girls anyway. I knew Kevin was disappointed but he just doesn't understand.

The girls were waiting for me out front of the club. The first thing that struck me as odd when we visited Diva's was that it was attached to an Econo Lodge. The foyer of the club was dark. There was no one around. We pushed the black double doors open. The neon lights were on around the T-shaped runway. There were gold floor to ceiling poles and fluorescent pictures on the walls of scantily clad women. The walls were painted purple. There were bar stools that lined the catwalk. A bouncer saw us and sent the manager over. He introduced himself as Mike. What's the deal with strip club managers named Mike? He offered us jobs immediately. So either he was hurting or he sent a spy to Delilah's to check out our routines. Mike gave us the phone number to reach Diva's house mom so we could give her our availability. He said we could start as soon as next week.

"Let's go out and shop for some new clothes" said Summer.

"I would love to but I really shouldn't. I have to meet Kevin at the realtor's office. We're going to try to buy the townhouse."

"Good for you" said Roxanne.

I kissed the girls Goodbye and went my own way stopping at Wawa for a fountain soda and a soft pretzel. I bought the same for Kevin as a surprise. He always did things like that for me. I made it to the appointment on time. That was a first. I'm normally always late. The realtor's name was Steve. He seemed nice. I kissed Kevin hello. Steve started us on the paperwork. He wanted basic information like date of birth, address, and proof of income.

"Oh no, I have no proof of income. I work in a cash only business. I have no W-2's or pay stubs."

I started to cry. I failed once again.

"I am really sorry, but without proof of income it will be especially hard to find someone to give us a mortgage."

"Wait, what if I apply for the mortgage?" offered Kevin.

"We can try," said Steve.

Kevin filled out all of the paperwork. Steve put Kevin's information into the computer. Kevin was approved immediately for $105,000.

"See, I told you everything was going to be okay. Now to get proof of income it looks like you're going to have to take the job at the hospital" Kevin said pleased at what he had just accomplished.

"I guess you're right."

It just sucked because I had debt. Those damn credit cards never asked you for proof of income. I called the ER manager and told her I would take the job. It was only one night a week and every other weekend. I could still work at the club one or two nights a week for extra cash and Diva's was so much closer then Delilah's.

"So, do you really want to live with me?"

"Of course I do. You're smart and beautiful. I just have one thing to ask: can we look at other houses. Let's just see what is out there.

So we could really get a new start. You know; fresh surroundings neighbors that won't vandalize your car."

"If you are referring to the crazy guy across the way he moved last month. But I guess it cannot hurt to see what else is out there" I answered.

We went back to the townhouse and made turkey and cheese sandwiches. It looks like we are going to be eating in a lot if we want to save for a house. Steve, the realtor called and said he had some listings he wanted us to see. Kevin had to stop by work and finish an arrest report. He dropped me off at the hospital to fill out employment papers. I was finished at the hospital before Kevin was finished at work so I called Roxanne to see what she was up to. She told me that tonight was preview night for a musical she was in at the community college. She told me they were performing Chicago. She asked if Kevin and I wanted to go. It sounded like fun. I told her we would absolutely be there to support her. Kevin came to pick me up and I told him about our plans for the evening. To my surprise, Kevin did not know what Chicago was about. In fact, he had never seen a musical at all.

We went back to the realtor's office and picked up Steve. The first place we went to see was a townhouse in Levittown. The section was a newer one. They looked nice from the outside. They had a pool and a work out facility. They were pluses. The one currently for sale was an end unit. That was good. Then you only have to worry about neighbors on one side of you. We walked inside. You had to go up about twenty stairs. When we reached the top I was greeted by pink carpet and stenciling everywhere. There was Ivy, flowers, hearts, even race cars in what I am guessing is their son's room. I could paint over the stenciling, not a problem. But then I looked out the window of the second floor landing and a problem arose. It was a direct view of the not so nice apartments next door. The townhouse was only separated from the apartments by a white vinyl fence. Yuck.

Moving on, we drove all of the way up to Holland. I really had never been there before. There was so much more to the area then I knew of. We entered a section called Village Shires. It was nice and quiet. The streets were tree lined. This development had three different pools and a gathering facility for residents. All of that did come with a monthly fee. The unit Steve took us to see was small. It was suppose to be a two bedroom and it was more like a one bedroom with an office. It did have nice sliding glass doors that led to an outdoor deck; perfect for a barbeque. The kitchen was also a good size. I didn't like the living room/dining room combo. I would probably just eat at the breakfast bar and make the living space larger. The last place we saw was in Langhorne. Holy flashback to the 1980's! There was wallpaper everywhere, even on the ceiling in some rooms. I am really not into paisley. The house was furbished with dark green carpets. The only area newer was the kitchen and that is probably because they had no choice if they wanted to sell. One thing I did love was the deck off of the kitchen. The yard backed to trees. It was nice and serene.

"So, what did you think?" asked Kevin.

"Honestly, I really like our place now. I love the fireplace and the cathedral ceilings. I love how quiet it is at night. I love that we have to do NOTHING to it. I love that the bedrooms each have their own bath. I love that we have a garage."

"Alright, I get the idea. Steve, give the landlord a call and get the ball rolling."

I jumped up and down and kissed Kevin. I didn't know what I would do without him. And I was getting out of having to pack. You can't beat that. Kevin and I went to Olive Garden to celebrate.

"The only thing I want to do to the townhouse is put a new kitchen floor in."

"That shouldn't be a problem, I'm a little handy."

"Are you excited about seeing the play?" I asked.

"Yes, I guess. What is it about again?"

"Okay; it's fast paced so I know you'll like it. It's a musical that's set in the 1920s. The plot switches between reality and the main character Roxie Hart's fantasies. The tale is about selfishness and murder. The storyline in Chicago focuses on the difference between being famous and having success. Roxie Hart is awaiting trial for murder. Her high profile attorney Billy Flynn has never lost a case. Billy Flynn and Roxie

Hart clash because they both love the spotlight. The difference is Billy

Flynn has success and fame, Roxie Hart has neither."

"Wow! That was a great description."

"It's one of my favorites."

We got to the theater and took seats right up front. I read the

playbill and I could not believe my eyes. Roxanne was playing Roxie

Hart. I had never seen that side of the blue eyed, raven haired girl. The

show began and she came out. Her makeup and hair were gorgeous.

She was so into her role. I kept smacking Kevin's arm saying

"Isn't this great?"

I bought Roxanne a bouquet of flowers for her performance. Roxie

Hart was such a great role for her to play. They were two people with

similar goals. Roxanne and Roxie shared the same characteristics. They

were both determined to succeed and have everything they wanted.

That didn't necessarily work out for Roxie Hart. Hopefully, Roxanne

will have a better shot. Roxanne came outside shortly after the show

was over. Her brother was waiting there.

"So, what did you think?" she asked with such enthusiasm.

"You were fabulous!" I gave her the flowers.

"Thank you."

Roxanne's brother was taking her out to eat.

"I'll see you later".

I was so happy for her. It was a great moment.

Kevin and I stopped at Goodnoe's for ice cream on the way home. We sat outside and talked.

"I know it doesn't seem like it sometimes but, I really do want so much to be happy. It's this fear I have of failing that is holding me back. I saw my parent's dysfunctional relationship; I guess I'm afraid I'll repeat the cycle."

"I understand. I just really wish you would let me in sometimes. This dysfunctional cycle you are so fearful of can end now with us. Hey, I really liked the play. Maybe for your birthday we will get tickets to a Broadway show" he offered.

"You are so sweet. That sounds great. We need a nice getaway."

Maybe we will break the cycle. I went to work at Delilah's the next day. During the lunch shift I handed out all of my invites to the new club. I hope my customers follow me up there. But, if they don't there will always be customers. Summer, Roxanne, and I were all working today. I think we had the same plan; to get our shit and get out. I got a box and started to pack my things. Ever since all of the drama with Craig, Delilah's hasn't been the same. Summer was right; it was time for a change. I came out of the locker room as she was making her rounds on the floor. I heard an older gray haired guy say,

"Honey, you need to get back to the gym and work on those abs."

The look on Summer's face was priceless. I thought she was going to poke his eyes out. Instead, she poured a drink in his lap. He called her a bitch. The bouncers picked him up and took him outside.

"Why are we always the bitches?" I said to Summer.

"Whatever makes them feel better." Summer said. Christy, our house mom entered the club.

"I am so sorry to do this to you, but I'm not going to be putting anymore time in."

"Effective when?" Christy asked sharply.

She was pissed.

"Today is my last day." I have to do what's best for me and right now that's to get out of here"

"I understand, one day I hope I will be gone to. It just sucks for me because now we are going to be short dancers" answered Christy.

"The customers will survive without us."

I finished cleaning out my locker, made my rounds, and said goodbye to everyone. No one asked me to stay. I think they could have cared less. I heard the manager say to Christy that strippers are a dime a dozen. I turned around and flung a dime at him. Roxanne, Summer and I walked out the door. That chapter in my life was closed. Maybe it was all of the anxiety but as soon as I got outside I puked my guts up. My throat started to burn when I vomited. That never happened before.

I came home and Kevin was still up waiting for me. I thought something was wrong.

"How much did you really want this house?" he asked.

"A lot, why?" I answered.

"Because we're going to OWN IT!" he screamed.

I shrieked and jumped up and down. I couldn't believe it. The landlord signed an agreement of sale. I'll be damned, Kevin was right. He said he would fix my problems and he did. We lit candles and laid in front of the fireplace in the living room.

"So, this place is going to be ours?"

"It sure, looks that way. Now, why don't you come over here and say thank you?"

I rolled over onto my stomach. Kev started to kiss the back of my neck. He took my shirt off. All of the sudden I felt COLD. He had gotten a piece of ice. He rubbed it along my neck and along my spine. He made my toes curl. He licked the water as it dripped down my back. He sucked on my fingers, kissed my arms all of the way back up to my neck. He rolled me over and started to kiss me and let the ice roll down my chest. It landed right into my belly button. He kissed around my belly and unzipped my jeans. He kissed my thighs, knees all of the way down to my ankles. I wanted to scream I was so excited. I couldn't help but to pull him on top of me. I grabbed a hold of him, he wrapped his arms around me and squeezed. If this is what love is like, count me in.

I wanted to get to school early the next morning. I had an anatomy and physiology test that I didn't really study for. I figured if I got to school early enough I would be forced to study with 45 minutes of time in before the test was administered. I pulled it off, so proud of myself. Things were going great. My cell rang, it was Roxanne. She wanted to know if I could come to Diva's, that she was working with Summer, and they were short a bartender for the lunch rush. I was done school for the day so why not make some extra cash? I could contribute to the house fund.

I was glad I went in. I needed to get to know the place. It takes me a while to feel comfortable in a new environment. I had a good time and met a lot of the customers. Diva's had a few more biker dudes then I was use to but it was alright. I noticed a lot of people using the breezeway between the hotel and the club and got the feeling the girls here did a little more than lap dances- if you know what I mean. I like to think I am pretty perceptive. Lunch was over and the kitchen had closed. I was wiping down the bar when Roxanne's regular, Jack came in.

"Hey, you came up here too?" asked Jack.

"Yes, we all came up here together. I guess you can call us a package deal."

"Can I get a cheese steak?" he asked.

"I think the grill is closed. Let me go check."

I went back into the kitchen and Jay, one of the cooks was complaining.

"What's wrong with you?" I asked.

"I freaking bust my ass back here and all I get is shit on" he answered.

"Sorry, anyway one of the customers is asking for a cheese steak. Do you think he can get one?"

"That depends, who is it?"

"It's that guy right there. I think his name is Jack."

"Oh no, I'm not cooking shit for that guy. He's the one that has a thing for Roxanne. He treats her like crap."

Jay spit on the grill and said,

"I'll cook him something, but it won't be a cheese steak."

"Okay, I'm just going to go pass that on to him."

I walked out of the kitchen and went over to Jack.

"I'm sorry Jack, but the grill is already turned off." Jack exploded. He threw his glass and started screaming at me.

"What the fuck do you mean the grill is closed? Do you know how much freaking money I spend in this place?"

I backed up behind the counter. Jack came around and pushed the register onto the floor. The register broke into pieces. It took three bouncers to get him outside. He was yelling something about being a big spender and how it was a bunch of shit that he couldn't get a freaking cheese steak. My chest started to hurt. I hadn't been that scared for a long time. It was the same way my dad use to rant when he was coming down from his high. Right before he would kick my ass.

The manager came over and asked me if I was okay.

"Physically I'm okay," I told him.

Roxanne came over and I told her what Jack had done.

"He couldn't have been that bad."

"Oh yes he was. You can keep him as your regular. I don't want any part of psycho man."

I was shaking. I needed to get the hell out of here. What the freak is the matter with people? I just don't get it sometimes. Do people actually think if they carry on and make an ass out of themselves they will get what they want?

Kevin had dinner on the table when I got home. He made the mistake of asking me about my day and told me to stay away from psycho man. Then he proceeded to tell me about a standoff that he was involved in at a local liquor store. So, I told him to stay away from drunks with guns.

"It's a deal. I've been thinking this is a great starter home. After you graduate nursing school and work for a little while we could get married, maybe have a baby?" Baby, I thought, I don't ever remember discussing babies. I can't keep myself out of trouble. Kevin really wanted to settle down. I hope I am not going to be a disappointment to him.

"You are making me nervous."

"Come on Amanda, you are too hard on yourself. Are you afraid you are going to turn out like your mom? Because if that's it you have already proven you can stand on your own. Your mother could never do that." Maybe he was right. Maybe I needed to just relax.

Kevin invited Nicole and Walt over to join us for a movie and desert. It was nice to see them. I enjoyed Nicole. She had such a positive perspective on things. Nicole said,

"Now that you guys bought this place Walt and I are going to look for something for us."

"That's great."

"Yes, we'll probably get married next year."

Kevin picked out a Freddie movie. I can't stand Freddie. He literally gives me nightmares. I had my eyes closed through half of the movie. Walt and Nicole were still hanging out after the movie was over. I was beat. I had to excuse myself. I went into the bedroom and fell asleep.

Diva's was having a bartending competition the following day. It was suppose to be a whole Tom Cruise, cocktail thing. I think the manager just wanted to see what we were capable of. I made sure I looked really good for the competition. I paid the DJ some extra cash to play the Tubes, She's a Beauty (One in a Million Girls). Everything was going great. A stripper I couldn't stand named Danielle decided she was going to go all Coyote Ugly on me. She pulled herself up and started dancing on the bar. I had no choice but to take the keg hose to her ass. The crowd went wild. She started screaming and ran into the locker room. She was a bitchy, customer stealer anyway. I was almost positive she was one of the girls that frequented the Econo Lodge for an additional fee. I had zero respect for her.

Kevin came by the club with his buddies. They had just finished up at the shooting range.

"Hey, you!" he said as I passed him some wings.

I filled two pitchers of beer for them and brought that over as well. Danielle must have noticed me paying special attention to Kevin because by the time I got back to the bar she was on his lap. He was a good sport for a second. She started to get a little fresh, he dumped her off of his lap and told her to move on. I think she was trying to get back at me for the beer shower. I looked over at her and blew her a kiss. She was pissed. I went about my business. Summer came up to the bar and said she just saw Danielle key my car. I could feel my face getting hot. I whipped around the bar and grabbed Danielle by her nasty red hair.

"You picked the wrong bitch to fuck with!"

I smashed her face into the bar. I did it a few more times until a bouncer she was friends with pulled me off of her. I haven't been that angry in a long time. It just makes me so freaking mad! I work hard to get the things I have and here comes this piece of shit who takes it upon herself to damage my property. At least I made quite an impression on her and everyone else for that matter. The customers started calling me Mad Mandy. It was cute at first, but it got old real quick.

"Yo, killer!" It's time to take you home." said Kevin.

Kevin and I went outside and saw that my car was scratched pretty badly.

"Don't worry. I can buff that right out."

I hope so; I hadn't even made my first payment yet. I boiled over my car the whole way home. Kevin had to work a double the following day. He always packed a bag when he worked like that. He was getting his things together. I decided to get my things together for school. We kissed each other good night and went to bed.

The next morning I went to school. My classes were great. I love it when my professor's keep me interested. I met up with Roxanne at the student union. We had lunch together. I told her what happened between Danielle and me. Roxanne does not know Danielle that well so she kept her opinion neutral. She is fair like that.

"Are you working tonight?" I asked.

"Yes, are you?"

"I'll be there" I answered.

I had some errands to run after school and had to go to the bank and get some things from the store. When I was done all of that I went home and cleaned the kitchen. I wanted to get everything ready to paint. I couldn't wait to redecorate. I felt so lucky having a place I can call my own. I have come a long way.

Chapter Nine

Jack-Just Call Him Jack

I parked in the Econo Lodge that night for work wanting to hide my car from Danielle. Grabbing my bag out of the trunk I walked around to the front of the club. Roxanne's crazy regular Jack was coming out of the Econo Lodge. I cringed and pretended not to see him. He came up to me and apologized for his behavior the other day. I flipped open the top on my mace. I wasn't taking any chances with him. I was shocked at the difference in his personality. Maybe he is bipolar and is off his medication?

"Really that wasn't me, it was the alcohol talking" Jack said.

Whatever, I wasn't letting that guy get any closer to me.

"I stay at the Econo Lodge because my wife doesn't want me to drive drunk."

Here's an idea, I thought to myself, then don't drink. But that would make too much sense. I could not get into the locker room quick enough.

"Hey Roxanne, I saw your Prince Charming in the parking lot. Did you know he was married?"

"His name is Jack, just call him Jack. And yes, I know he is married, Amanda" she answered.

"What is that crap about him staying at the Econo Lodge?" I asked.

"His wife probably makes him stay out so she can get a break from him." Roxanne answered.

We laughed. Danielle wasn't working tonight so I could let my guard down. The club was slow. We weren't making a lot of money. All of the girls who were done decided to go shoot some pool. I asked Roxanne to come with us. We have fun when just the girls hang out. Roxanne wanted to stay. She walked out to the parking lot with me. We ran into Lexy outside. Roxanne got in the car with her and I left. I went to the bar. The girls and I hung out and smoked some weed. It helped relieve some of my anxiety. It was getting late and I headed home. Kevin was asleep when I came in. I crawled into bed and crashed.

I was late for class the next morning. To make things even worse we had a "pop" quiz in Anatomy and Physiology. It would have helped if I did my homework but who has the time for homework? I was so upset with myself after class I went to the student union for a latte but didn't see Roxanne. I chatted with a few other people I knew before going home really needing to sleep. I don't know what was wrong with me. I had been getting so easily exhausted lately. There was a message on the answering machine from the emergency room manager. She wanted me to call her back to schedule some training shifts. I did promise Kev

I would take the job so, I called her back. Mary seemed happy to hear

from me. That was good. I wanted to make sure that I didn't just get

the job because of Kevin. I called Summer to tell her about my new job.

She was excited for me until I told her where I would be working.

"Oh my God, Anthony's father is a nurse in that ER!" said Summer.

"Oh well, he's not going to know that we know each other unless

you or I tell him. I won't say a word." Then Summer had an idea.

"I know what you can do; you can spy on Carlos for me. You see

Carlos doesn't like to pay child support. He always cries poor. I am sure

that Carlos is far from poor but I can never prove it. So now you can

give me the dates when he is working overtime."

"You are a real bitch! I'm glad I don't have those problems."

We hung up and I called Roxanne's cell to see if she was re-

cooperating from last night, but she didn't answer. I left her a message.

I took a nap and when Kevin came home we went out to celebrate my

new job.

"Do you really think I will be okay at this?" I asked Kevin.

"You'll be fine. I do think you have self esteem issues."

"Knock it off."

"No, really, I'm so proud of you." He made me feel good.

I was twenty minutes early for my first training shift in the

emergency room. Sure enough, Summer's ex was there. Another nurse had told Carlos she saw a news special on the Rabinowitz case. Carlos said,

"It's a real shame that they couldn't charge Summer with anything in relation to Craig's wife's murder. You know she never did come out and tell me she was a stripper before all of this happened. I had my suspicions though. All of the nice things she was buying. My son is always in designer clothes."

I could not believe how right on Summer was about this guy. A nurse named Anna was going to train me, she introduced herself. She was very nice and asked me if I had any experience. I told her no. She asked me where I worked previously and my stomach started to hurt. I told her I was a going to school for nursing and that this is my first real job. She was satisfied with that, thank God. I didn't know if I could handle any additional questions. Anna wanted me to shadow her and get a feel for the place. It was a good thing. I just basically followed her around. I saw where things were kept and met the other staff members.

When I was done working I couldn't wait to get to my car and call Summer. Her ex really is an ass. I told Summer about the conversation I overheard. She laughed and said,

"Didn't you believe me when I told you how he is? Now you know it is not just me? He is not a very nice person. Have you heard from Roxanne? Her brother showed up at Diva's looking for her."

"Roxanne probably just needed a break from everyone. She'll turn up."

I stayed in once I got home. I had to do some reading for school. I had to start paying more attention if I wanted to pass my classes. Besides, I wanted to hang out and spend some quality time with Kevin.

The next morning the phone rang before the alarm even went off. It was Kevin.

"Hey, what are you doing?"

"What do you think I am doing? I'm still in bed. I have 20 minutes left to lay here. Why what's up?"

"Just stay right there, I'm coming home. I will explain when I get there."

I got up and turned the tea pot on, put a bagel in the toaster, and got my things together for class. Kevin came into the kitchen with the paper rolled up in his hands.

"Hey, come over here and sit down."

"Kevin, what's wrong? You're beginning to scare me."

I sat down and he unrolled the paper. Roxanne's picture was on the front page. Then I read the headline:

Woman Found Dead Under Turnpike Bridge.

My chest started to hurt. I couldn't breathe. I got a sharp pain in the back of my head.

"What happened?" I asked.

"They don't know yet." answered Kevin.

I skimmed the article as much as I could without getting more upset. Two kids riding quads along the shore in New Jersey found her body.

"Who would do such a thing? Who would kill her? She wouldn't hurt a fly."

"When is the last time you saw her?"Kevin asked.

"Two nights ago at the club. When I left she was with Lexy."

"You guys may have been the last people to see her alive. We need to contact the detective who is running the case."

I was going to vomit. I rocked back and forth on the floor in the bathroom. Kevin made a few phone calls. He wanted me to go meet with the detective running the case. I got into the shower and began to sob. I felt so horrible. I should have stayed until I knew she was safe. Did she know the person who did this to her? Was she afraid? Did Lexy see anything? My mind was going a mile a minute. I thought so hard but I didn't remember anything out of the ordinary. Nothing was standing out in my mind. Kneeling in the shower, I let the scorching water run over me. It was so hot the bathroom filled with steam. Kevin came in to check on me. He pulled me out of the shower, wrapped a warm towel around me and hugged me.

"It is going to be okay. They will find who did this to her."

"I know; it's just like a bad dream."

I went into the bedroom to lay down. It felt like I couldn't function. I couldn't believe she was dead. When I finished getting dressed we went to the police station to see if we could be of any help. The detective there was not very nice. He kept asking me the same questions over and over.

"When was the last time you saw Ms Siani? Who was with her? What color was the car? What clothes did she have on? Was there anyone suspicious around?"

I guess he wanted to make sure my answers did not change. Two hours later we walked out of the police station.

"I want to see where they found her."

"Are you sure you want to go there? It may not be the best thing for you right now. It might just upset you more."

"I feel like I have to go and see for myself."

We drove across the turnpike bridge. It was exactly two minutes from where I left her. How scary is that? The area was still roped off with crime scene tape. The grass was high in some places and in other spots there were clearings. I got out of the car and walked for a while. I looked up at how high the bridge stands. That must have been horrifying for her. She was lying here alone for days. My heart ached for her. She may have made some bad decisions but she was a good person.

The ride home was quiet. Kevin stopped and got me water ice and a pretzel. He was bugging me to eat and didn't want me to get sick. All I could think about was that there is a psycho out there who killed my friend. What if he saw me? What if he thinks I know something?

What if he comes looking for me? I was making myself insane. I asked Kevin if he cared that I was going to quit Diva's. There was no way I was ever going back there.

"I have to tell you, I'm glad you're going to stop dancing but I do wish it was under different circumstances. Roxanne was alright."

I called and told the manager to take me off of the schedule. He told me he understood and to call if I changed my mind. That wasn't going to happen. I went home and tried to concentrate on school work. Did you ever try to read and all you saw were letters on a page? You know, like you couldn't absorb the words? That is how I felt. Kevin brought me a cup of tea and sat down beside me.

"I can still hear her giggling when she said goodbye.".

"It's a hard thing that you are going through. My dad died when I was 14 and I remember having similar feelings. It's hard when someone dies before their time. Look, I know one of the guys in the department. He promised to call me as soon as there was an update on the case."

Kevin stayed home the rest of the day with me. I was quiet, I felt like I didn't have anything to say. I wasn't scheduled to be anywhere in the morning and tried to distract myself by looking through paint colors and sale ads. It didn't work. I just couldn't shake this feeling of sadness. I did some wash and bummed around the house. Then the phone rang. It was the detective that Kevin was telling me about. He said they were interviewing a local drifter and some employee from

Diva's in relation to Roxanne's murder. I knew the one guy he was talking about and he was crazy but harmless. I didn't want to tell the detective that. I will let him do his job. I am sure he would figure it out on his own.

Friday was my first day back to school after Roxanne's death. It was hard walking by the student union knowing she would never meet me for coffee again. I was scheduled to work at the hospital that afternoon. Hopefully, that will keep my mind off of things. Kevin brought me soup from my favorite country store. I think he just wanted to check on me at work. The girls at the hospital were teasing me. They said they loved it when I was here because if they needed the police the response time would be two seconds instead of twenty minutes. I laughed. The hospital staff was so nice. They invited me out for drinks with them. Maybe I did need to surround myself with different people. We went to the bar next door to the hospital. We sang karaoke and drank beers. This one nurse, her name was Shannon, man she could carry a tune. She missed her calling as a pro singer. I got to know the girls a little better. They were all young moms that were married and lived in the area. It was like they had taken me under their wing. I felt like I had known them for years. Kevin showed up and got me from the bar. Roxanne's funeral was in the morning. We needed to get to bed.

It was a warm and sunny day. Kevin drove me to Roxanne's viewing. Roxanne was only her stage name. Her birth name was Rachel Siani.

But she liked the name Roxanne. She thought it was fun, sexy. Her viewing was very quiet. Her brother made a great speech. Rachel's dad and step-mom were standing together. I couldn't stay. I started to feel like I couldn't breathe. My palms started to itch. My eyes wouldn't stop tearing. I pulled on Kev's jacket. I told him it was time to go. When we got into the car Kev's cell was ringing. It was the detective in charge of Roxanne's case. He had questions about Roxanne's customer Jack. John "Jack" Denofa was a professional sign painter who lived in Bucks County. He had a strange relationship with his wife and a nasty temper. That was all I knew. The detective claimed that they had a description of a vehicle they believed was carrying Roxanne's body onto the bridge. The vehicle description was that of a red Dodge Ram pickup. It matched a truck owned by John Denofa.

"Oh my God Hon, Jack was at the Econo Lodge that night! Do you think he was waiting outside for her? Do you think he killed her in a drunken rage?"

"Relax; the cops know what they're doing. They'll get a search warrant for the truck and search the hotel room he stayed in."

At least they were going to pick him up for questioning.

It comforted me to know that the cops were on the right track. Roxanne's murder was not a random act of violence. Jack intentionally killed her. That bastard! I knew he was no good. He reminded me too much of my dad. I told her to stay away from him. Roxanne was quiet for the most part. You could never really tell what she was thinking. I will tell you this-I know she didn't think he would kill her.

We met some friends from Kevin's work at a local sports bar. I didn't drink any alcohol at all, I wasn't in the mood. Kevin was telling people if they showed up in the ER while I was working that they better be nice to me. I smiled, not over what has happened but, at least now I was able to deal with it.

I worked in the ER the next day training with Anna in the triage area. This is where patients are seen when they first come into the emergency room. Can I tell you that when someone called me to say they were in the ER I was always like

"Oh My God, what happened?"

Now that I am working in an ER that whole attitude has changed. This woman came in drinking a Mountain Dew and eating Doritos. Her complaint was abdominal pain. The nurse politely asked

"What brings you here today?"

This lady said,

"I have had this pain in my stomach for two months and I'm here today because I want to know what's causing the pain."

I took the patient's vital signs and gave them to Anna so she could chart them. I heard Anna tell the patient she is to have nothing more to eat or drink until the physician examines her. Anna then sent the patient to be registered out front. We watched the patient on the close circuit TV continue to eat her Doritos and drink her Mountain Dew. Anna just rolled her eyes.

"I don't know why I bother."

Just then, two police officers come in with a patient who needed medical clearance for incarceration.

"Anna, what do they mean?" I asked.

"Basically it's a paper that says the prisoner is in good health. It's also so the prisoner cannot say that the cops beat him up before they took him to prison."

The ER doctor looked the person in custody over and asked him if he had any complaints before he would sign.

"Go in there and get a baseline set of vitals on the person they brought in." Anna said.

I must have looked nervous because she continued on with,

"It's okay, he's in handcuffs and the officers will stay with him."

I couldn't believe Kevin did this for a living. I almost died when I walked into the room. It was John Denofa in handcuffs! I was so afraid he was going to tell everyone that I use to be a stripper. But Jack acted like he didn't even know me. Maybe he didn't recognize me because he was sober? The longer I was in his presence, the longer I was frustrated. I couldn't believe Jack. He was laughing and joking with the officers. You would have thought they were good old friends. That piece of shit. It took all of the strength I had not to spit in his face. I wanted so badly to ask him if it made him feel like a man when he threw Roxanne from the bridge. The cops were talking to Jack about sports and what he does for a living. I wanted to vomit. I heard them say that when they left the hospital Jack was going to be arraigned. I prayed that bail wouldn't be awarded. I went home that night so pissed off. I told Kevin I was afraid Jack was going to get away with murder.

"Why do you say that?" he asked.

I told him how nice the cops were to him. They were laughing and telling jokes.

"You idiot, that is all an act. The cops were nice to him so he would let his guard down and maybe slip them some information about the murder that they previously did not know."

"That's kind of sneaky, you really can't trust anyone."

I was still disappointed when we turned on the 11 o'clock news and saw that Jack was given bail. What made it worse was that he was able to post his $500,000 bail. His family put their home up as collateral. Jack was claiming that he was framed. How was he sleeping at night? If I was his wife, his ass would be sitting in that jail cell until trial started. I would be damned if I was going to sign over my house for a worthless piece of scum sucking trash like that.

Chapter 10
I Have A Problem

Kevin and I were off together the following day. It was a day we had been long waiting for as it was the date we make settlement. Surprisingly enough the settlement went very smooth. I had a doctor's appointment afterwards because I hadn't been feeling well. I wanted to make sure I wasn't getting run down with all of the stress I'd been under lately. The doctor sent me for some labs and told me to start taking vitamins.

When we got in the car Kevin shocked me with a pamphlet on bulimia.

"I picked this up in the doctor's office. Amanda, I really think you have a problem. It's not just me, other people have noticed. You do get sick a lot. You need to read this and we need to get you help."

"How dare you! I don't have a problem. Just because my stomach is upset easily I'm all of a sudden bulimic? I am not in high school!"

"No, you are not, but you do have self esteem issues."

"Screw you! You don't know what you're talking about."

Needless to say the car ride home was quiet after that. I ran into the house and locked myself in the bedroom. We should have been celebrating the house. Now, he owns it. He could kick me out if he wants and again, I would have no place to go. We weren't committed to each other. We weren't married. What the hell was I going to do now? I rolled over and saw the pamphlet on the floor and wondered where he got the idea that I would be bulimic. I started to page through the brochure.

What is Bulimia?

Bulimia, also called bulimia nervosa, is a psychological eating disorder. Bulimia is characterized by episodes of binge-eating followed by vomiting to control your weight. Vomiting is an inappropriate method to control your weight. Other Inappropriate methods of weight control include: fasting, enemas, excessive use of laxatives and diuretics, or compulsive exercising. Excessive shape and weight concerns are also characteristics of bulimia. A binge is an episode where an individual eats a much larger amount of food than most people would in a similar situation. Binge eating is not a response to intense hunger. It is usually a response to depression, stress, or low self esteem issues. During the binge episode, the individual experiences a loss of control. However, the sense of a loss of control is also followed by a short-lived calmness. The calmness is often followed by a period of unhappiness. The cycle of overeating and purging usually becomes an obsession and is repeated often. Bulimia was only diagnosed as its own eating disorder in the 1980s. People with bulimia can look perfectly normal. Most of them are of a normal body weight, and some may be overweight. Women with bulimia tend to be high achievers. It is often difficult to determine whether a person is suffering from Bulimia. This occurs because bingeing and purging is often done in secret. Also, those individuals suffering from Bulimia often deny their condition. Sufferers consume huge quantities of food. Sometimes up to 20,000 calories at a time. The foods on which they binge tend to be sweet foods, high in calories, or smooth, soft foods like ice cream, cake, and pastry. An individual may binge anywhere from twice a day to several times daily.

A Family Member has an Eating Disorder

If you have a family member with an Eating Disorder, your family member needs a lot of support. Suggest that your family member see an eating disorder expert. Be prepared for denial, resistance, and even anger. A doctor and/or a counselor can help them battle their eating disorder.

What Causes Bulimia?

There is currently no definite known cause of bulimia. Researchers believe it begins with dissatisfaction of the person's body and extreme concern with body size and shape. Usually individuals suffering from bulimia have low self-esteem, feelings of helplessness and a fear of becoming fat

Medical complications from bulimia?

Some of the most common complications of bulimia are: Erosion of tooth enamel because of repeated exposure to acidic gastric contents. Dental cavities, sensitivity to hot or cold food, swelling and soreness in the salivary glands (from repeated vomiting). stomach ulcers. Ruptures of the stomach and esophagus, abnormal buildup of fluid in the intestines. disruption in the normal bowel release function, electrolyte imbalance, dehydration, irregular heartbeat and in severe cases heart attack, a greater risk for suicidal behavior, decrease in libido.

Symptoms of Bulimia?

Some of the most common symptoms of bulimia are: Eating uncontrollably, Purging, Strict dieting, Fasting, Vigorous exercise, Vomiting or abusing laxatives or diuretics in an attempt to lose weight, vomiting blood, using the bathroom frequently after meals, preoccupation with body weight, depression or mood swings. Feeling out of control, swollen glands in neck and face, heartburn, bloating, indigestion, constipation, irregular periods, dental problems, sore throat, weakness, exhaustion, bloodshot eyes.

Risk Factors of Bulimia

There are certain professions where eating orders are more prevalent. Thinness is usually emphasized in: modeling, dancing, gymnastics, wrestling, and long-distance running.

Good news about Bulimia?

Bulimia can be overcome.

Was Kevin right? Just because I had a few of these symptoms, was I sick? Just then there was a knock on the bedroom door. It was Kevin with a piece offering.

"Look Amanda, I know I was tough on you but it's only because I care. Can you at least think about going to talk to someone?"

"I guess it couldn't hurt."

"I really don't want to fight with you about this," said Kevin."Can we just move forward from here and get you taken care of?"

"I think that sounds like a plan." I answered.

A week went by. I got a call from the doctor to come in for an appointment. Kevin came with me. I had figured that we were going to talk about the possibility of bulimia. Boy did I get a shock. The doctor's office told me I was pregnant.

"Pregnant, Oh my God, this is great!"He hugged me and kissed me.

I was just kind of stunned. I wasn't sure how I felt. I wasn't sad, but I wasn't ecstatic; probably because it wasn't planned. Kevin brought up the possibility of an eating disorder with the doctor.

"Now that you're pregnant, you need to remain in good health. You need to eat right, take prenatal vitamins and have plenty of fluid. If you don't your baby could be malnourished and you may not be able to produce breast milk" said the doctor.

"I understand. I will do everything I can to keep this baby safe and healthy."

"Good that is what I want to hear, said the doctor. Now you need to follow up with an OB/GYN and they can take care of you during your pregnancy. They will weigh you and if you are still losing weight you may need supplements and extra fluid."

We no sooner left the doctor's office and Kevin was on the phone with his mom. He was very excited. I smiled but I was very anxious inside. I wasn't sure if I would be a good mom. I worry so much. I don't have a stable home life. I am still not over the death of my friend.

"Let's go shop at the baby store around the corner" Kevin said.

"If you want to" I answered.

"What's the matter Amanda?"

"I'm okay, still in shock I guess."

"Yes, but it's a good shock. We'll be fine. I really don't want you losing any more weight though. Will you tell me if you get the urge to vomit before you do it, please?"

"I will, I promise."

Kevin was like a kid in a candy store, only it was a baby store. He filled a shopping cart with sleepers, blankets and bottles.

"Don't you think our families will have a shower for us?" I asked.

"Yes, but I want to buy so things now!" replied Kevin.

He was scaring me. I know he loved me but I still had doubts about this whole thing. Kevin was working the night shift so he got ready to leave as soon as we came home. He put me on the couch with a blanket, a drink and the phone, kissed me on the forehead, and practically skipped out the front door. As soon as he was gone I called Lindsey and Summer to come over. I needed to have a pow-wow. Summer got to the house first. She was all smiles.

"What's up?" she asked.

"Why do you think something is up? Can't I just want to see my friends?"

"You know you have been a little hard to reach since everything happened with Roxanne. What's going on?"

"Well, I was going to wait until Lindsey got here to tell you, but, I'm pregnant."

"Pregnant, are you sure?"

"Yes, the doctor confirmed it with blood work."

"So, how do you feel about that? How does Kevin feel about it?"

"He is ecstatic. He already called his mom. I, on the other hand, am really not sure how I feel at all about this."

"Well, I have to tell you that I had my son when I was young. I ended up a single parent and it is hard. But, I wouldn't have it any other way. I love my little guy".

Summer and I went for a walk down the trail. We ended up at the park, watching the kids play. I think she was right. You have to take responsibility for your actions. So my lifestyle changes a little. I saw Lindsey coming down the walk and waved her over. Summer was leaving. She had to get to work. Hopefully, she too will change her career after all of the drama. Besides, you cannot strip forever. Lindsey sat down on the bench next to me. I caught her out of the corner of my eye starring at me. It was like she was waiting for a bomb to drop.

"I'm pregnant."

"You are? What are you going to do?""I don't know. Summer had some good points."

"Summer? Why the hell would you listen to her? She is so wrapped up in herself and what she thinks is right that she will never do any good for anyone else. You need to have an abortion right away."

"What? You know my mom is raising my daughter because I was so young. I was pregnant with Chuck's child when I caught him with that other girl. I had an abortion as soon as I got back from California."

"I never knew. Why didn't you tell me all of this was going on? Maybe I could have helped you in some way."

"No, Amanda. There was nothing anyone else could have done for me. There was no way I was bringing a child into all of that."

"Did Chuck ever know? Do you regret it?"

"No, I never did tell Chuck. I was going to surprise him when we got back from our trip. But he ended up being the one who surprised me. Do I regret it? Sometimes, especially when I see these kids playing. I think I could have been a good mom without Chuck. But, all in all, I believe I did was what best."

"Wow that is a lot to absorb.".

"You're not kidding; try being the one who lived it. I see my mom raising Kayla and I wish I could just take her back. But I know I can't. It is not right. Kayla has a life with her and I respect that. We all need to move on. I got a new job at the hospital."

"You did, That's great. What are you going to be doing?"

"It's a secretarial position, but it is a start" Lindsey answered."

"I am so proud of you. I knew you could do better things."

"Alright, I have to go. My mom and Kayla are taking me out to dinner to celebrate my new job. I'll call you later. I'll see you. Congratulations!"

Hmmm.... I had a lot to think about. I couldn't believe Lindsey opened up to me after all of this time. And Summer, I'm kind of impressed with how her main priority is her son. I need to go see my grandmother. I walked back to the townhouse and drove over to the cemetery where she was buried. It was only 20 minutes from my house. I hadn't been there since her funeral last May. It looked like someone had been there recently. There were fresh flowers. I missed her, Oh God did I miss her. I wondered if my life would be any different if she were still alive. She would know what to do. After all, she raised me for my first five years because my mom was only 16 when she had me. That was my grandmother. She would take charge if she needed to. I remembered her telling me that there was no way she was going to let my mother give me away,I was a part of the family and she wasn't going to let me go without a fight. My grandmother was a devoted catholic so abortion was out of the question. I was still struggling with my beliefs. This seems to be another test of faith for me. I was not comfortable with the idea of abortion. I didn't feel I had a right to take away a life, but what kind of life could I give a child right now? I vowed I would not let my own children grown up how I did. Eating frozen pizza and living in a two bedroom, run down house in a not so nice area of town. I have love to give, which is more than my parents had for me, but will it be enough?

Chapter Eleven

Fairytales Don't Always Come True

In the meantime, Jack was brought back to court for trial. He had the audacity to tell the press that he had been keeping himself busy with family and business. I wanted to know how his family could look at him. Then again his wife did allow him to attend strip clubs on a regular basis. I was in court every day. I had to listen to them trash Roxanne. The defense said she was troubled; aren't we all troubled? And they portrayed Jack as a loving family man who only spent time at the clubs to entertain his customers. Whatever! It was hard hearing the details from the coroner. He believed that Roxanne was beaten and strangled in Jack's hotel room. So, Roxanne must have seen Jack after I left her with Lexy. I am guessing she went back to his hotel room and that is when they had a fight. Jack was probably drunk and got violent with her. The coroner said that Roxanne was injured from the attack, but that was not what killed her. Jack then threw her out his hotel window into the back of his red Dodge Ram pickup and drove her to the New Jersey side of the turnpike bridge. It wasn't until she was thrown 112 feet from the turnpike bridge that she died. I couldn't even imagine what she went through before she died. I hope she was out cold, I hope she hadn't suffered. I'd seen firsthand how violent Jack could be in a drunken rage. I knew it was him, he killed her. That made me crazy. The defense was on my nerves, trying to claim that someone stole Jack's pickup truck and used it to dispose of Roxanne's body. I was so happy that the court saw right through Jack's made up defense and convicted him to thirty years to life in prison with no chance of parole. They took him away in cuffs from the courthouse right over to county lock up. The smirk was finally gone from his face.

I came home from court exhausted that day. There was a woman on my front step. She told me her name was Maria and that she and Kevin have been having an affair for months.

"Why are you telling me this?" I asked her.

"Don't get me wrong, I don't want to hurt you. I just thought you should know."

"If you didn't want to hurt me you wouldn't have had an affair with a taken man in the first place, Bitch! Get the fuck out of here before I kick your ass!"

I was hysterical. I felt my heart break into pieces. How could this happen? I couldn't get my key into the front door, I was shaking so badly. I gathered up all of Kevin's things and put them into trash bags. I put the trash bags on the curb. I called for a locksmith to come change the locks before Kevin came home from work. I called both Lindsey and Summer. Summer was at work, but Lindsey came right over.

"I knew he was an ass. I thought he was way too possessive of you. Now we know it was because he was the one cheating the whole time."

"You're not helping, Lindsey. I need a plan. Kevin comes home in three hours. Maybe sooner if that chic called and told him what she did."

"See, I told you that you should have had an abortion. Now look, you are going to be stuck raising this kid by yourself. Men aren't worth all the drama. I am back on my feet and I'll move back in and help you with the mortgage."

"Kevin owns this place Lindsey; remember I couldn't get a mortgage?"

"Well, then you come stay at my house. Let's get your things."

Just then Kevin came home and demanded to know what was going on. I opened the window and screamed,

"Why don't you ask Maria?"

Kevin's color went from red to pale. He insisted that it was a one time thing and that she didn't mean anything to him.

"That was real funny because she meant a hell of a lot to me."

"I don't know what you're bitching about. The whole thing was your fault! You were so wrapped up in finding Roxanne's killer that you forgot all about me!"

"Are you freaking kidding me? You are out of your mind. If that is your excuse then you need to go you selfish piece of shit!"

"I will go, but I'll be back. Just remember who owns this place."

I fell onto my bed and cried. I'll just max out my student loans and get my own place. I can do this and I'll be fine. I'm strong, but I was so hurt. This can't be happening, not now. How could he do this to me after everything we have been through? I had to get my mind off of this so I turned on the TV. They news was reporting that Jack's conviction had been overturned. Jack's defense council filed a motion saying that Jack deserves a new trial in New Jersey because of something called territorial jurisdiction. The defense believed because the coroner testified that Roxanne died when she hit the ground in New Jersey, not in the hotel room in Pennsylvania, charges should be dismissed immediately and a new trial should be granted in New Jersey.

Kevin had blindsided me with all of this crap and now Jack was going free. Chalk up another bad day for me. I was glad I had a doctor's appointment in the morning, I felt so sick and started to vomit. In my heart I did not want to throw up but I couldn't stop myself. I called Lindsey and asked her to pick me up a milkshake. Lindsey came right over and hung out with me for the rest of the night. It was like old times.

The doctor was concerned because I had lost three pounds. I told him it was because I had been under a lot of stress lately. My doctor said next time, if I lose any more weight I am going to the hospital to be admitted. I promised him I would do better. From the look on his face I am not sure he believed me. He wanted me to come back in a week for a weight check. That was fair. Kevin was there when I exited the doctor's office.

"How are you and my baby?" Kevin asked.

"Everything is fine and you need to leave me alone. I can't handle this right now."

"Amanda, I want you to stay in the house. I want you to be taken care of. If you need me, I'm staying with my mother."

Kevin walked with me to my car and tried to kiss me. I put my head down and shut the door. I saw him in my rear view mirror as I drove away. I just didn't understand. If he loves me so much why did he do this to me?

When I got home there were flowers on the front steps and a note from Kevin. The note said that he didn't know why he did what he did. He also knew that was not an excuse. Kevin says he was with that woman twice and that one night while he was watching me sleep he realized how wrong he was. He said it was when he broke it off that she threatened to tell me. He wanted another chance.

I was not sure about that. I always swore that once a cheat, always a cheat. I turned the tea pot on and sat in front of the TV with the paper. There was an article that read John "Jack" Denofa settled a wrongful death suit with Roxanne's family. They didn't waste any time, did they? It's a shame because she wasn't even that close to her dad and step mother. What are you going to do? Hopefully they put the money to good use. Maybe they will use it to raise awareness of domestic violence. That would be nice.

My next shift the girls at work surprised me with a baby shower. They were so sweet. The shower was huge! There was gifts and food. I got everything I needed and more for the baby. I was happy and so relieved knowing I couldn't afford everything I needed by myself. After the shower the girls went to the local hardware store and picked out paint for the nursery. We got pizza and came back to the townhouse for a paint party. The girls helped paint and decorate the nursery. I picked a Noah's ark theme. I think that's what I will name him, Noah. It was a good strong name. It was also different, so he'll stand out. We finished up the decorating touches with a border and lots of stuffed animals. The girls nominated me for a nursing scholarship so I have no other choice but to finish school. It was so nice to have a group of people who cared about me and didn't owe them anything. They didn't want anything from me except for me to be happy. Maybe I wasn't so lost after all.

The next day I visited the site Roxanne was found. I put flowers down and I told her that I would make sure Jack goes to jail for a very long time. I will be at his next court date and will make sure she gets justice. I also gave her an update on everything that was going on with me. She would have freaked if she found out Kevin was cheating on me. She never did say either way if she liked him or not. And a baby, I can hear her now. She would have never pegged me as the mother type.

I kept up on school and still worked my shifts at the hospital. It kept me busy. Kevin and I had worked out an arrangement. I would pay the utilities and he would pay the mortgage. We would reevaluate the situation after the baby came. I had met someone else in the meantime. There was a paramedic at the hospital, his name was Joe.

Joe and I started spending time together. He knew my story and he hung out with me anyway. I thought that was brave. Kevin and Joe weren't friends but the paramedics sometimes do need to request the police to assist them on a call. He was taking a chance spending time with me. He took me out to eat and helped me clean the house and would even help me study for school. He was a really nice guy that helped take my mind off of Kevin. But now with a baby I knew Kevin would never be far away.

My pregnancy was going well. I was gaining weight, too much weight. I finally had a great support team and good friends. Maybe God does bring you to it to guide you through it. Maybe he was trying to get me to learn from my experience? Maybe all of this would make sense to me some day.

Work offered me a class to become a counselor for victims of domestic violence. I jumped on the chance, and loved helping other people. I had a good ear and a lot of background with domestic violence. If I was able to break the cycle anyone can. I was so excited when I received my certification. I would now be called into work when a victim of domestic violence and/or a violent crime came in as a patient. My job was to stay with them and make sure they were comfortable. I could offer them resources for coping and healing. After everything I had been through I never lost sight of myself, realizing now how important that was. I wanted to share that with others and also learned a lot I didn't know about domestic violence in the class. I thought there was just physical and emotional abuse. I did not realize all of the other aspects.

What is Domestic Violence?

Domestic Violence is a pattern of abusive and coercive behaviors, including physical, sexual, and psychological attacks, as well as economic. Adults or adolescents use these things against their partners for the purpose of gaining power and control over them. Domestic violence is lethal, common, and affects people of all cultures, religions, ages, sexual orientations, educational backgrounds and income levels. Domestic Violence is a crime and can include the following types of abuse:

Physical Abuse: The abuser's physical attacks or aggressive behavior can range from bruising to murder. It often begins with what is excused as minor contact that escalates into more frequent and serious attacks. Physical abuse includes behavior like: pushing, shoving, slapping, damaging property or valued items. They may leave their partner in a dangerous place, or they may refuse to provide assistance when their partner is sick or injured. Psychological and/or Emotional Abuse: Psychological or mental violence can include anything that impacts the mental health and well being of the partner, such as: name-calling, constant criticism, harassment. The partner may blame the victim for everything. They may be excessively possessive and jealous. They may isolate the victim from family and friends. They may use intimidation and humiliation.

Sexual Abuse: Physical attacks by the abuser is often accompanied by sexual violence wherein the victim is forced to have sexual intercourse with the abuser or take part in unwanted sexual activity, including unprotected sex.

Economical Abuse: This includes any behavior that maintains power and control over finances, such as: preventing their partner from getting or keeping a job, making their partner ask for money for every expense, limiting partner's access to funds and limiting the partner's knowledge of family finances; therefore controlling their funds.

Am I being abused?

It can be difficult to acknowledge that you or someone you care about is involved in an abusive relationship. Domestic Violence does not look the same in all relationships; however, there are some warning signs that may indicate you are in an unhealthy relationship. Take a few minutes to answer these questions:

- Does your partner insult you in public or in front of your kids?
- Does your partner treat you like you are stupid or call you names?
- Does your partner try to control what you do?
- Does your partner act really jealous of your friends or family?
- Does your partner blame you for his/her violence?
- Has your partner ever threatened to hurt you or themselves if the relationship ends?

If the answer is yes for one or more of the questions, it is important for you to get help.

Leaving an abusive relationship

Domestic violence hurts the entire family, leaving an abusive relationship is not always easy. The victim may be deeply in love with the abuser. They may hope the situation is going to change. They may feel guilty about breaking the relationship up, especially if they have children together. In other cases, the person may be scared to leave because of the abuser's threatening or harassing behavior. Leaving becomes even more difficult if the victim does not have a job or the support of family and friends to start a new independent life.

It was only one day before I was called in on my first case. The victim was an older woman. She had been beaten by her husband because she didn't have dinner on the table in time. He had plunged a fork into her left cheek. It was horrifying to me. I didn't understand violence and it threw me even more when I saw the actual damage it did. I can't tell you her name but I can tell you she had a tiny build and a quiet voice. She was very timid and rarely made eye contact with me. She asked me why I cared about her. I told her that I had a friend who was a victim of domestic violence. Her abuser eventually killed her.

"I want the abuse to stop. No one deserves to be treated like that," I said.

It was my scheduled weekend to work. I began to check my supplies as usual when all of a sudden my water broke. The emergency room staff called 911 because they didn't deliver babies there. Boy, were they frantic. Kevin must have heard the call go out because he came flying through the bay doors. It had been a while since we last spoke. He kissed me on the forehead and told me he was never leaving my side again. I wasn't in a position to argue. I had a lights and siren escort all the way to labor and delivery. I think we made it to the other hospital in ten minutes. The poor security guard couldn't get me to labor and delivery fast enough. The sweat was beading on his forehead. Two and a half hours later, we met Noah. He was perfect. He had ten fingers and ten toes. He weighed in at eight pounds, eleven ounces, and he was twenty inches long. I held him tightly in my arms. He was so precious, he wrapped his fingers around my pinky.

About a half hour after he was born, my doctor and the nurse left us alone. Kevin fell asleep in the chair. I was watching Noah sleep when the TV caught my attention. The New Jersey Supreme Court declined Jack's request for a new trial. The court re-instated his original sentence and conviction. Jack was now awaiting transportation to a state facility where he would spend the next thirty years to life. It was a long time coming. I felt so overwhelmed. I started to cry. I guess sometimes in order to start over you need to let it all go.

If you or someone you know is in a violent relationship, or is planning to leave one, it is important to make a safety plan. If you do not have friends or family close to you right now, you can always speak to a crisis intervention counselor.

If you or someone you know is suffering from bulimia, please contact a family physician or guidance counselor for help. Please do not suffer in silence. There are people here for you. They can help you like they helped me.

CPSIA information can be obtained
at www.ICGtesting.com
Printed in the USA
BVOW03s0215100217

475849BV00015B/127/P